G·B·TIEPOLO

BY ANTONIO MORASSI

PHAIDON

G·B·TIEPOLO

BY ANTONIO MORASSI

I. TIEPOLO'S SELF-PORTRAIT AT THE AGE OF FIFTY-SEVEN, WITH HIS SON DOMENICO. 1753
Detail from the ceiling fresco in the Residenz at Würzburg. Cf. Plate 68

G·B·TIEPOLO

HIS LIFE AND WORK

BY ANTONIO MORASSI

WITH 180 ILLUSTRATIONS

LONDON · PHAIDON PRESS · 1955

MADE IN GREAT BRITAIN

TEXT AND HALF-TONE ILLUSTRATIONS PRINTED BY HUNT BARNARD AND CO LTD · AYLESBURY · BUCKS

PHOTOGRAVURE PLATES PRINTED BY CLARKE AND SHERWELL LTD · NORTHAMPTON

COLOUR PLATES PRINTED BY LUND HUMPHRIES AND CO LTD · BRADFORD

DUST JACKET DESIGNED BY RENÉ BEN SUSSAN · PARIS

BOUND BY KEY AND WHITING LTD · LONDON

CONTENTS

TO THE MEMORY OF
GIULIO LORENZETTI

PREFACE

GIAMBATTISTA TIEPOLO, *born in 1696, began his career as a painter at about the age of twenty; that is, about the year 1716. Since he continued to work uninterruptedly until his death, which took place in 1770, his active career spans more than half a century—fifty-five years, to be exact. His activity was enormous. He painted sacred and secular subjects on large and small canvases, histories and mythologies, genre scenes and portraits, and, above all, frescoes. Fresco painting was indeed his native element, where he felt himself to be the conductor of an orchestra and where his imagination could take flight in the harmonies which he created.*

The vastness of Tiepolo's output appears almost immeasurable. Alternating the painting of frescoes with easel pictures, he worked by himself or with the aid of insignificant collaborators (with the exception, of course, of the specialist Mengozzi-Colonna in the perspective and ornamental parts) until about 1745, after which time he had the valuable help of his son Domenico, and, rather later, that of his less able son, Lorenzo. The individuality of the two sons, however, was entirely submerged when they were working for their father, in his style and under his direction. They were in fact part of the Tiepolo firm, be it said with all respect, and during his lifetime 'Tiepolo' meant Giambattista. Tiepolo was always overwhelmed with work and his pressing commissions gave him no rest; he frequently lamented the fatigues of his life in letters to his friends, fatigues which, as 'orders', compelled him in his old age to travel to Spain. As he himself wrote, he had to obey chi può comandare *and here it is not difficult to observe the shadow of the political designs of the Republic of S. Mark making use of the artistic embassy of Tiepolo to further its diplomatic relations with the Court of Spain, which had indicated its desire that Tiepolo should decorate the new Royal Palace with frescoes.*

Giambattista never stayed for long in Venice. As a young man he went to Udine, Milan, Bergamo, Vicenza and the towns of the Terraferma to decorate churches, palaces and villas; later on he spent three years in Würzburg and then eight in Madrid, and, at the same time, he was supplying canvases to the courts of Bavaria, Franconia, Prussia, Saxony, Spain and Russia.

All this may give an idea of the size of his output, and it is obvious that so vast an œuvre cannot be compressed in the limits of a single book such as this, and so it was decided to divide the material. This volume contains the critical introduction, with the most important facts on Tiepolo's works and places him against the background of the art of his time; then follow a bibliography of the essential books, and notes on the plates. The plates themselves, obviously, can be no more than a selection from the most important works of the master, but they are intended—and this was the specific desire of the publisher—to give an impression of the complexity and variety, the high level of quality, lightness of form and airy transparence of colour, which characterize the art of the man who was justly considered the last of the great Venetians. Another volume, addressing itself to those who want to study the Master's complete œuvre in greater detail, will contain the Catalogue Raisonné of Tiepolo's works with numerous illustrations and will give details of technique and history, with critical, chronological and bibliographical remarks. This Catalogue will also include paintings which are by his sons, pupils or imitators, but have been wrongly attributed to Giambattista himself. The two volumes together will form a true corpus of Tiepolo's works.

This corpus, the result of many years of study, is intended to make the artist known to a wider circle and also to re-establish the original purity of his œuvre—to liberate it, that is, from the superstructure of false ascriptions and 'false readings'; to define it within exact limits of time and to establish the stages of his chronology (always an essential task in the understanding of the development of any artist); and, finally, to add those early works, from the period when he was still relatively Tenebrist, works which were once given to Piazzetta, Ricci or other minor artists—to anyone, in fact, except their true author.

The conception of Tiepolo's art which obtained until a few decades ago was a rather curious one: it consisted of a restricted idea, often a lack of understanding, of his early period, while being expansionist—sometimes as all-embracing as the Divine Mercy—in everything else. The word Tiepolesque then meant, roughly speaking, all of those paintings of the eighteenth century in Venice (and often they were not even Venetian) which contained even an echo or a reflection of Tiepolo's style or the type of subject favoured by him. There were occasions when all that was needed was for a small picture to have a glimpse of sky between clouds, and a few angels or putti in flight to evoke the name of Tiepolo when really it was, at best, a work by a pupil, a follower, or an imitator, such as Giovanni Raggi, Giustino Menescardi, Giulio Cesare Ligari, Francesco Chiaruttini, Bernardino Bison, Francesco Fontebasso, Fabio Canal and so on; while in the worst cases, the painters responsible for these pictures fathered on the great Venetian were anonymous daubers of the last century.

★　　★　　★

It is not possible for me to mention here all those who have helped me in one way or another during the preparation of this book: their names are recorded, with the expression of my gratitude, in the Preface to the Catalogue volume.

Nevertheless, it seems to me unfair not to make at least a mention of those people who have been most intimately concerned in the preparation of this book: apart from Dr B. Horovitz, his indefatigable assistant Dr I. Grafe; Mr and Mrs Peter Murray, who undertook the far from easy task of translating the Italian text and were also prodigal with helpful suggestions; and also Signora Dr Mercedes Precerutti-Garberi, my constant and unfailing helper. My deep and sincere thanks to all of them.

A. M.

INTRODUCTION

TIEPOLO is not a member of that company of artists misunderstood in their own times. Indeed, so fully did he realize the ideals of the eighteenth century, and with such vivacity and imaginative power, that the whole of Europe – with the possible exception of France – saw in him the great standard-bearer of contemporary painting. It is no coincidence that from about 1736, when he was invited to go to Sweden, until 1760, when he went to Madrid, every Court of the age competed for his works.

It may be said at once that the fact that he was loaded with the highest honours during his lifetime should not be held against him. There is, nowadays, a certain type of criticism which seeks to uphold the risky thesis that an artist's greatness is in inverse relation to his popularity among his contemporaries; but this is a thesis which applies only in a few extraordinary cases and as an exception. Certainly, there was a short period of almost total lack of understanding of painting from about 1870 until about 1910 – that is, from the Impressionists to the first Cubists – but no one would think of denying that since then every effort has been made towards a critical revaluation of the period, and that the importance of these artists, and of some living artists, has often been exaggerated, occasionally beyond their due.

As for the old masters, the greatest among them were understood and celebrated in their own life-times, from Giotto to Titian, van Eyck to Rembrandt, and Dürer to Velazquez. Even some of the more original and strange, such as the elder Bruegel, Bosch, Grünewald, El Greco and Goya, were well enough understood by their contemporaries; and so was the much discussed Caravaggio, who received commissions from Princes and Cardinals, and if he was not given more it was because of his demoniac personality, which led to his premature death.

We know, however, that Giambattista Tiepolo's character was mild, good-natured and accommodating. The Swedish Minister, Count Tessin, wrote to his King, who had instructed him to find a suitable painter to decorate the new Royal Palace at Stockholm: 'Tiepolo, dit Tiepoletto, est fait exprès pour nous . . . il est plein d'esprit, accomodant comme un Taraval, un feu infini, un coloris éclatant, et d'une vitesse surprenante. Il fait un tableau en moins de temps qu'il en faut à un autre pour broyer ses couleurs . . .' It is obvious that Tessin, a man of taste and a connoisseur of painting, regarded the Venetian as an ideal artist; and it is a fact that, from the very beginning, Tiepolo embodied in himself all the current artistic ideals of the age, and at the same time, he revived Venetian painting, giving it substance, naturalness and light. Between 1720 and 1730 he gained the ascendency over all other Italian painters, from Crespi to Piazzetta, Magnasco to Ricci, Solimena to Giaquinto. In 1726 he was referred to as 'celebrated' by the Board of Works of the Cathedral at Udine, when they commissioned the frescoes in the Chapel of the Sacrament. He was then thirty years of age.

To such a brilliant beginning there corresponded a career rich in artistic experience, strivings and problems. Close study of the grand ascending curve of his art reveals how frequently he strove to outdo himself or to renew the springs of his inspiration. Count Algarotti, his friend and adviser – but whose advice, it may be observed in passing, was not always useful to the painter – called him 'a great connoisseur of styles'; and it is beyond question that in his boundless production there are phases of influence, sometimes transitory, sometimes merely an impression, from other artists, such as Veronese, Piazzetta, Ricci and even Rembrandt, but each suggestion lasted only a short time and was assimilated, consumed by his creative fire.

There can be no doubt that Tiepolo's art rapidly conquered the taste of his time. Goethe himself, who at heart detested the Baroque, could not restrain his admiration for Tiepolo's frescoes in the Villa Valmarana at Vicenza, for he wrote to Frau von Stein that the artist was to be seen there 'gar fröhlich und brav'; and this was in 1786, when Tiepolo was dead and Neo-classicism had swept all before it. We may well ask ourselves why Tiepolo's success was so rapid. His own age saw in him an instinctive pictorial power, a bold and astonishing creative ardour. Even when using Piazzetta's type of dramatic chiaroscuro, Giambattista showed formidable powers, and when, at the age of nineteen (in 1715) he painted in the church of the Ospedaletto, it was immediately apparent that his work there surpassed that of his Venetian contemporaries in the originality of his pictorial ideas. From this type of painting, still *tenebroso,* Tiepolo passed swiftly and decisively to the conquest of light, and from the Udine frescoes (1725 onwards) light meant to Tiepolo something different from the bland, pale illumination of the *chiaristi* of his day – of an Amigoni, a Pellegrini, a Dorigny or any other minor painter – becoming vivid, vibrant and, above all, full of sunlight. Lanzi observed justly that Giambattista 'using dull colours immediately next to a few clear touches, gave his pictures a vivacity . . . a sunlight, which perhaps has no equal'. This was the first element in his success, for it must be borne in mind that in the seventeenth century and the first decades of the eighteenth, Italian painting was preponderantly Tenebrist, and, therefore, the need for light, for the sun, became compelling.

The second factor which raised Tiepolo's painting above the level of his contemporaries was his spectacular illusionistic power, achieved through a consummate mastery of linear perspective and an equally amazing grasp of aerial perspective. When one thinks of the perspective illusionism of a Padre Pozzo, a Bibiena, a Bacciccia, they seem,

II. ALEXANDER AND CAMPASPE IN THE STUDIO OF APELLES. Canvas, about 1725. Montreal, Museum of Fine Arts

by comparison with the skies of Tiepolo, heavy and inflated machines, while Giambattista's ceilings in churches and in the rooms and staircases of palaces open up into a splendour of iridescent light, where the figures lose all weight and are swept up among the clouds into infinite space; they are transformed into music and become, as it were, atmospheric poetry. The realization of this new world of painting obviously presupposes an incessant study of the human form, articulated in an inexhaustible variety of movements and in an infinite gradation of light; above all, it requires an uncanny pictorial intuition.

The third factor in his success was the raising of the status of fresco painting, often reduced in the seventeenth and early eighteenth centuries to a secondary, decorative role; inferior, that is, to easel painting. Tiepolo raised it once more to the high artistic rank it had held in the Golden Age of the Cinquecento. Abandoning the amorphous characterizations, full of mannerisms, of the seventeenth century, and far surpassing the example of his contemporaries, Giambattista introduced into his pictures figures taken from life, portraits, men of flesh and blood instead of mere puppets – and what power of dramatic imagination, and how new and heroic the spirit which inspires these figures !

Even in his earliest works one is astonished by the liveliness of his figures, endowed with a nervous energy rendered more acute through the closest study of movement, in a dazzling play of light and shade, reflections, foreshortenings and pictorial devices which have no like in the painting of the period. To this must be added Tiepolo's ability to create with his frescoes a complete and all-pervading harmony. His painting fits into the architectural setting, and often it was only painted architecture, with such a harmonious sense of proportion, with such a balanced and delicate freshness of colour, that it creates a vivifying and joyous atmosphere, in which each part has its exact counterpart, as in a well put together piece of music. That this pictorial phenomenon should arise in the city of Benedetto Marcello and Antonio Vivaldi in the century of Bach and Mozart, will surprise no one who is aware of the links which bind these two great imaginative arts. The 'musical' fusion of painting with its surrounding architecture was already established in Roman Baroque, and this fusion played its part in Tiepolo's development. To this was joined the type of stage design practised by the Bibiena family, from whose circle came the perspectivist Gerolamo Mengozzi-Colonna, Tiepolo's collaborator in the ornamental and perspective parts of his decorations. In Giambattista's hands these elements were translated into a far higher harmony and a far greater degree of perception – a perception of crystalline clarity.

Tiepolo appeared, however, to his contemporaries as the man who revealed new ideas, new horizons, and this position he held almost until the end. Only in his last years was his fame obscured by the art of Mengs, and even more, by the intrigues of the Spanish Court, which profoundly embittered him. And at the moment of his death Neo-classical painting, then in the ascendant, had come – more from preconceived ideas than from inner necessity, from the study of archaeology and of ancient literature – to dominate art with its precise and rationalistic dogmatism derived from the theories of Winckelmann.

Thus, during the whole Neo-classic period, which lasted for more than a hundred years, the art of Tiepolo, and with it the Baroque world, remained under a cloud. Only towards the end of the last century was interest re-awakened in the work of the master, after a few painters, like Delacroix, had already been struck by its grandeur and spirit, and, later still, the Impressionists had admired its clarity and transparency, precursors of the *plein air*. Slowly its revaluation began. This revaluation coincided, in fact, with the whole process of critical revision of the Baroque – due above all to Riegl and to Dvořák – which focused art-historical studies at the beginning of this century with a new historical objectivity on the examination of this period, one of the most imaginative and exhilarating ever known in the history of art.

But the question must be asked whether Tiepolo was really a Baroque painter? Without doubt, he was at the beginning, when he composed complex figure masses full of dramatic pathos and strong contrasts of light and shadow, but in his strivings towards perfection he soon sought to reach a point of balance, of measure, and finally of such a rarified poetry of light that his personality transcends the definition of Baroque. The gestures of his figures, too, which at the beginning were violent and immoderate became more controlled, yet still charged with an exuberant, though restrained, vitality, so that by 1735–40 his art can better be defined as Classic, in the sense of measured serenity and coherent perfection, rather than Baroque. His contemporaries saw in him a Classic artist for they acclaimed him as such – as a *Paolo Veronese redivivo* (for example, in the short poem in his honour written after the unveiling of the frescoes in the Palazzo Clerici at Milan in 1740) – and recognized in him the heir and restorer of the great Venetian Renaissance tradition. It is clear that the names given to different periods of artistic activity, and even the division into periods of an activity which was, and is, a ceaseless stream of human creation, can have only an approximate value, though such names have their uses for practical and methodological purposes. This means that the term Classic is equally inadequate to characterize Tiepolo's art which is Classic in a way of its own, reshaping Baroque to its own ends and for that reason, like all the highest creations of the mind, it escapes rigorous definition. But one thing is certain: it is not Neo-classical. The personality of Tiepolo is passionate and instinctive, exuberant, sensual or pathetic, according to his theme; it is restrained, but never frigid, the opposite of the chill rationalism of Neo-classicism. This explains why to the Neo-classics, the theorists, the academics of the late eighteenth and the nineteenth centuries, the art of the great Venetian was a closed book.

4

But his revaluation, which went hand in hand with the discovery of light by the French *plein air* painters of the last decades of the nineteenth century, has been rapid. After various critical studies by Italian, French and German writers, the first notable monograph on Tiepolo appeared in 1896. It was by Chennevières, and he was soon followed by Meissner (1897), by Modern (1902) and then in 1909 by Molmenti's important book, and in 1910 by the very fully documented work by Sack, these last two books being milestones in the historiography of Tiepolo and remaining to this day sources of the first rank.

Nevertheless, whoever turns the pages of these two monographs, now over forty years old, quickly realizes that they are defective in two points: primarily on Tiepolo's early period, and then on the distinction between his works and those of his son Domenico. The early period was not deeply studied then, because it was, to a certain extent, foreign to the ideas of luminosity which were responsible for the artist's return to favour. As to the distinction between father and son, the point of departure was then the presupposed absolute inferiority of the son, and thus to Domenico were ascribed, as a matter of principle, those works which were not of sufficiently high quality to be assigned to Giambattista, and from this several serious confusions have arisen. To these deficiencies must be added the lack of chronological precision. This is not a negligible matter for anyone who wishes to get to the bottom of the problems of the artist's development, for without an exact knowledge of the chronology the study of an artist, as of a whole artistic period, can only be haphazard.

In these last decades the history of art has succeeded in adding two new chapters to the life of Tiepolo: one, at the beginning, on his youth, which was tumultuous, spent in ceaseless experiment, full of *Sturm und Drang*; and another chapter at the end on Domenico. But this last chapter assumes such an importance that it forms in its turn a book on its own; Domenico, in fact, must be considered not only as continuing the art of his father, but also as an independent personality turning towards genre painting illustrating aspects of daily life in Venice, and sometimes mocking at it with unforgettable caricatures, like Hogarth or Rowlandson. Thus enriched by the rediscovery of the works of his youth, with the works which are not his, or which should be restored to Domenico or assigned to other artists eliminated, and with the chronology properly established, the figure of Giambattista appears more distinctly and coherently in its stupendous development, and his work, which covers more than a half century of uninterrupted activity, shines out the clearer.

Fig. 1. THE SACRIFICE OF ABRAHAM. About 1715–16.
Venice, Chiesa dell'Ospedaletto

Fig. 2. THE REPUDIATION OF HAGAR. 1717–19. Milan, Conte Rasini Collection

Fig. 3. THE MARTYRDOM OF SAINT BARTHOLOMEW. About 1721. Venice, Chiesa di S. Stae

Fig. 4. MADONNA DEL CARMELO. About 1720–22. Milan, Brera

I

THE EARLY YEARS:
THE FIRST WORKS IN VENICE AND UDINE

1715 – 1730

WHEN Giambattista Tiepolo was born in Venice, in March 1696 (probably on the 5th), the son of Orsola and Domenico, co-proprietor of a merchant vessel, it was at a moment in Venetian painting when the sun was setting on a century weary, insignificant and inglorious. The epoch of the Bellini, Carpaccio, Giorgione, Titian, Veronese, Tintoretto was now far away and almost a myth. To these great figures had succeeded, at best, Palma Giovane, Vassillacchi (l'Aliense), Pietro della Vecchia, Marescalchi, Loth, Liss, Forabosco, Strozzi, Maffei . . . and these last were not even Venetians.

Giambattista was barely a year old, when his father died, leaving a modest competency to his widow, who now alone had to bring up six young children. The little Giambattista was soon placed in the school of Gregorio Lazzarini, a painter then well thought of, living in the same parish of S. Pietro in Castello as the Tiepolo family. From Lazzarini, an able designer of vast figure compositions, the young artist learned above all that which was then called the *mestiere,* that is, the mechanical part of painting – drawing, perspective and composition. But he also learned there a certain grandiose decorative manner, a certain predilection for iridescent effects of colour, which was to return more strongly in later years, and above all he learned how to manage with bravura complex groups of figures in vast pictorial compositions.

But Lazzarini belonged to the old school, the school of Seicentisti which included such painters as Zanchi, Maffei, Celesti – sound men, but not sufficiently exciting to satisfy a spirit as restless as the young Tiepolo. In fact, it was not long before he perceived that the traditional formulae of his master were not enough for him; he therefore left the studio of Lazzarini and set up for himself, and with that eager desire which characterizes the most fervent imaginations, with that curiosity which stimulates all original research he absorbed everything in contemporary Venetian painting which he could turn to good use. The well-informed Gianantonio Moschini said of him (in 1809) that 'eager to imitate whatever was popular in his own day, he emulated now the showy manner of Bencovich, now the strong shadowings of Piazzetta'. In particular, the latter impressed the young Tiepolo by the dramatic power of his chiaroscuro, derived from Giuseppe Maria Crespi and from various precedents in the Bolognese school. As to Federico Bencovich, called Federighetto, it is clear that certain intensely expressive attitudes – almost grotesque – in some of the early works of Tiepolo, go back to ideas inspired by the Dalmatian. But it may be seen that he added to these the fat and fluent colour of Sebastiano Ricci, the nervous energy of Magnasco, the tasteful, classicizing arcadianism of Carpioni and others.

In these formative years of his *Sturm und Drang,* years tormented by the effort of finding his proper bent, it is natural that Tiepolo should have looked for support now here, now there, watching his contemporaries. We must try to understand the feelings of this restless youth, only half satisfied with what he found in contemporary art, and it may have been that even then his spirit turned, as to a profound source of strength, to the works of the *Patres Patriae* of Venetian painting – Tintoretto and Titian, and then to Veronese. Through such contacts, he was, in later years, able to take over the great historical function of Venetian painting.

Giambattista was exceptionally precocious. Independent at about eighteen, when he was twenty-one, in 1717, he was already inscribed in the *Fraglia* (guild or confraternity) of Venetian painters. At nineteen he had already received an official commission to paint over the niches in the Church of the Ospedaletto. This is stated explicitly by Da Canal in his Life of Lazzarini of 1732, which provides some precious information about his chief pupil. 'Tiepolo,' he wrote, 'now so famous, was a pupil of his, notwithstanding that he abandoned his master's painstaking manner, inasmuch as, all spirit and fire, he adopted one resolute and rapid. This may be seen in the Apostles, which, at the age of nineteen, he painted over the niches of the church of the Ospedaletto.'

In calling these figures Apostles, Da Canal's memory is at fault, since they must be identified instead (as everyone is now agreed) with the two figures of the *Sacrifice of Abraham,* which he confuses with those of apostles and prophets by other painters. The form of the arch, over which the canvas has been inserted, cramped the composition and forced Tiepolo to use exaggeratedly strained and distorted poses for his figures, in the showy manner of Bencovich. But the impetuous touch, the saturated and fat colour, the vivid effect of light, already endow this painting with the flavour of modernity, and place it, by comparison with the other paintings in the same series in this church, executed at about the same time (1715–16), on a higher and more modern plane (Fig. 1).

The painter's preference for composing on a diagonal, for large masses in violent contrasts of light and shadow (an inheritance from the seventeenth century, revived by the contact with Piazzetta) is especially manifest in the *Repudiation of Hagar,* in the Rasini Coll., Milan, a work of 1717 or 1719 – a date which can be read with the signature on the stick in the bottom right hand corner. Here too, as in the Isaac of the *Sacrifice,* the figure of Hagar, though so violently bent as to form almost an angle, yet remains within the unity of the composition by reason of the interplay of strong light and shadow, linking the woman cast upon the ground with the majestic figure of the patriarch, built up, if one may so express it, over a void of deep shadows (Fig. 2).

Giambattista was twenty, or a little more, when he painted this canvas; and he was exactly twenty years old when he painted, in competition with other artists, a 'Pharaoh submerged' – that is, a *Crossing of the Red Sea* – a work which was 'applauded when it was exhibited on S. Roch's day' as Da Canal records. (These exhibitions took place in public, in front of the church and the Scuola di S. Rocco, as may be seen in Canaletto's famous picture in the National Gallery, London, and because of this first public success, Tiepolo retained a special devotion to the Pilgrim Saint, whom he painted in many small votive pictures.) Again in competition with other artists, he painted, towards 1721, for the church of S. Stae, a *Martyrdom of S. Bartholomew*, imbuing the martyr, whose dramatic lighting and searing agony dominate the whole scene, with a violence which had no precedent except in Tintoretto. Every line is contorted in restless agitation, in ceaseless undulations, and the vivid light is not treated drily, but in soft, almost liquid transitions, so that, in its handling, the work reminds one of some of the chromatic effects used by Liss. Among the works of his competitors his stands out as the most lively and the most essentially original. The huge canvas of the *Madonna del Carmelo with souls in Purgatory*, recorded by Da Canal and by Zanetti, and now in the Brera, dates from shortly after the *S. Bartholomew*. The principal group of the Madonna is placed, strangely, towards the right, and the whole composition appears unbalanced until one remembers that the canvas was designed to be seen foreshortened, since it was originally placed on the right wall of the choir of S. Aponal. Tiepolo carefully calculated the perspective effect of the composition and endowed it with a monumentality of planning and breadth of pictorial design that must have given the measure of the great future before the young artist (Figs. 3, 4).

Soon he had important commissions. Probably the first official commission for a fresco in Venice itself was for the vault of the side chapel in the church of the Scalzi, where he painted the *Glory of S. Theresa*. This work, which from its style may be dated about 1720–25, is most important, since it provides the key to the understanding of Tiepolo's secrets in the representation of his 'heavens', the mechanics, as it were, of his perspective. Still working within the great Baroque tradition, the artist here establishes some new principles which were to become the rule in the further development of his perspective decorations. The way in which the artist gives prominence to the principal group, drawing it clear of the tangible plane of the wall, and tying it, by means of the clusters of musicians in the second plane, to the throng of angels above the painted allegorical statues at the sides, is certainly his own invention. In a whirlpool of clouds rising in ever narrowing circles towards the zenith, Tiepolo places on high, upside down and seen in the most daring foreshortening from below, the angel who, offering the martyr's crown to the Saint, makes the depth of the vortex fully apparent. In the execution of this fresco, Giambattista has as collaborator in the perspective and ornamental parts, as we know from Zanetti, the Bolognese Gerolamo Mengozzi-Colonna, who remained his faithful companion until the departure for Spain in 1762; and it must be admitted that part at least of Tiepolo's perspective virtuosity is due to this consummate *quadraturista,* heir to the Bibiena tradition (Fig. 5).

After so early and so amazing a start, Giambattista must quickly have climbed the ladder of fame. A number of canvases, medium or small in size, as well as the much larger ones already mentioned, enable us to follow step by step, from his very earliest years, the stages of his formation as a painter of easel pictures as well as of frescoes. Of particular significance for his earliest period are the four canvases of mythological subjects now in the Accademia at Venice, which for so long were misattributed – *Diana and Callisto, Diana and Actaeon, Apollo and Marsyas* and the *Rape of Europa.* The artist is at home among the compositional schemes of a Ricci or a Solimena, although the sense of space and light is much more lively and acute in him. There is a greater play of restless lines, a vibration of unusual colours, vivid and sharp, contrasting with large areas of unassertive half-tones or heightened in the most important parts to an almost dazzling violence, which presage already the great impresario of the future. Some of the figures are types pushed almost to the point of caricature, and certain nude figures clearly recall Carpioni. Yet in all the works of this period, Tiepolo displays the quality of his originality in spite of the obvious signs of his conscious efforts to find new means of expression. This may be seen in the little canvas of *Diana and Actaeon,* which has all the flavour of a sketch, or in the *Rape of the Sabines* in the Museum, Helsinki, which is the *modelletto* (a small sketch prepared for the approval of the commissioner) for the large canvas in Leningrad, or in the *Jugurtha before the Roman Consul* in the Marinotti Coll. in Milan, the *modelletto* for the huge canvas in the Baltimore Museum. With what an exquisite touch Tiepolo knew how to play upon the strings of his pictorial instrument may be seen in the delightful little canvas of *Venus with a Mirror* (Pl. 1) or in the equally enchanting scene, certainly of the same date, of the *Temptation of S. Antony* (Pl. 11) in the Brera, compositions which share a flavour of that open sensuality inherent in the epoch. The drawings of this period show the inborn pictorial sense of the young artist. They are fairly rare, because often misattributed, but in them one finds now a study of linear movement, now an unravelling of figures in a complicated composition, or again a closely knit play of light and shadow, as in the *S. Jerome* in the Museum at Bassano, dashed off with an exaggeratedly forceful touch (Figs. 6-8).

Church commissions were rapidly followed by others for private persons. Da Canal relates in detail how Doge Cornaro entrusted Tiepolo with the direction of the pictorial

Fig. 5. THE GLORY OF SAINT THERESA. Fresco, about 1720–25. Venice, Chiesa degli Scalzi

Fig. 6. THE RAPE OF EUROPA. About 1720–22. Venice, Accademia

Fig. 7. THE RAPE OF THE SABINES. About 1720–22. Helsinki, Museum

Fig. 8. JUGURTHA BEFORE THE ROMAN CONSUL. About 1722–25. Milan, Marinotti Collection

Fig. 9. ALLEGORY OF THE POWER OF ELOQUENCE. Sketch for Palazzo Sandi, about 1724–25. Zurich, Private Collection

Fig. 10. ALLEGORY OF THE POWER OF ELOQUENCE. Ceiling fresco, about 1724–25. Venice, Palazzo Sandi

Fig. 11. ULYSSES DISCOVERING ACHILLES AMONG THE DAUGHTERS OF LYCOMEDES; APOLLO AND MARSYAS; HERCULES AND ANTAEUS. About 1725. Castelgomberto, Conte da Schio Collection

Fig. 12. ETEOCLES AND POLYNICES; HANNIBAL CONTEMPLATING THE SEVERED HEAD OF HASDRUBAL. About 1725–30. Vienna, Kunsthistorisches Museum

works in his palace at San Polo, which later passed to the Mocenigo, – works which must have been executed before 1722, when Doge Cornaro died; but nothing remains of these works since the building was completely transformed in the last century. On the other hand, the decorations, in fresco as well as on canvas, which Giambattista executed in the Palazzo Sandi a Corte dell'Albero, do survive and these, equally, are vouched for by the same biographer. Since the palace was built between 1721 and 1725, and since in the following year Tiepolo was in Udine, one must conclude that he executed these decorations in 1725, if not a year or two earlier. We may infer a date shortly before 1725 for the ceiling fresco from the *modello* recently discovered in Zurich, which is very closely related to the four mythologies in the Accademia. On this ceiling Tiepolo developed the theme of the *Power of Eloquence,* by means of four mythological episodes; *Orpheus reclaiming Eurydice from Hades, Amphion's music raising the walls of Thebes, Perseus on Pegasus killing the monster,* and *Hercules and the chained Cercopes,* while in the centre of the ceiling, in the luminous depths of the sky, he portrayed *Minerva, Protectress of the Arts, and Mercury.* Here we see again his characteristic faces, heavy and just a little vulgar, with popping round eyes, and the heaviness in the contorted limbs of the figures which recalls his earliest works; in fact, some of the fumblings of inexperience in a composition in which the individual incidents are not perfectly fused. But the young fresco painter's heroic style is already in full development and the white Pegasus, a neighing stallion overflowing with strength, wings spread to the winds – prototype of hundreds of horses which Tiepolo will launch across his mythological skies – would alone suffice to call down the Genius of the revived Italian painting on the young artist (Figs. 9, 10).

The decoration of the room was completed by Tiepolo with three canvases on the walls, now belonging to the Conte da Schio at Castelgomberto, near Vicenza. The largest represents *Ulysses discovering Achilles among the daughters of Lycomedes,* the two smaller *Hercules and Antaeus* and *Apollo and Marsyas,* compositions which are a bit confused with echoes from the seventeenth century of Loth and Langetti, yet with passages here and there of an astonishing painterliness in a *matière* all life and fire, and full of promises of things to come (Fig. 11).

These promises were soon kept, with the ten vast canvases furnished for the Ca' Dolfin in Venice, two of which, one of *Eteocles and Polynices,* the other of *Hannibal* are now in the Kunsthistorisches Museum in Vienna, or with the magnificent cycles of frescoes painted for the Palace of the Patriarch Dolfin, now the Archiepiscopal Palace in Udine. These frescoes, executed from about 1725 to 1728, at about the same time as the ten canvases for the Venetian palace, are the masterpiece of Tiepolo's youth. Their critical evaluation is, however, quite recent, since the Baroque elements which are still important in these works prevented them from being considered in their true light by the critics of Tiepolo at the end of the nineteenth century and the beginning of this one. And if there were still some who could not bring themselves to admit that Giambattista was the painter of the whole cycle, which they wanted to assign in part to his collaborators or to other artists, they were wrong, as I have been able to show elsewhere, and as is now universally admitted (Fig. 12).

In 1726 we know that Tiepolo was called to decorate the chapel of the Holy Sacrament in the Cathedral at Udine with frescoes, and in the documents he is referred to as 'celebrated'. From a letter of the time, dated 30th July 1725, we learn that the Patriarch Dolfin 'is making a staircase in the Patriarchate the like of which will not be found anywhere in Italy.' Since this letter certainly refers to the pictures and not to the architecture of the staircase, which is mediocre, it may be argued that the artist began his work in that year – 1725 – that he interrupted it to do the frescoes in the Cathedral in 1726, and that he took it up again immediately after. In the ceiling of the staircase Tiepolo frescoed a *Fall of the Rebel Angels,* clearly derived from Roman and Bolognese sources, with a Lucifer hurled upside down, outside the frame moulding (the hand and part of the drapery are modelled in stucco), giving the illusion of the figures detaching themselves from the 'tactile' surface of the ceiling. If, here, the connections with other Baroque fresco painters (Pozzo, Bibiena, Giordano, Ricci) are evident, in the paintings in the Gallery the artist has succeeded in creating something completely new, a landmark in the painting of the century.

In the central medallion of the Gallery ceiling he painted a fresco of the *Sacrifice of Abraham* (Pl. 2) which has nothing in common with the picture done ten years earlier for the church of the Ospedaletto; it is an airy composition, lively and liquid in handling and transparent in colour, like the other two subjects – *Hagar in the desert* and the *Dream of Jacob* – thrown up on to the same ceiling in what appears to be a rather off-hand way. On the walls, Tiepolo represented three stories from the Old Testament corresponding to the three ovals on the ceiling: on the left is the *Angel appearing to Sara,* (Pls. 6, 8) in the centre *Rachel hiding the idols* (Pls. 3-5), and on the right the *Angels appearing to Abraham* (Pls. 7, 9). The scenes are filled with a new sunny atmosphere. The figure of Sara is an example of a portrait in the manner of Veronese in accordance with contemporary taste, and is a very early example of his influence – a portrait of an old, vivacious, toothless woman, silhouetted against the light behind her as if caught by the beam of a searchlight which makes her greenish-blue flesh tones almost vitreous; the unforgettable angel has one rosy, fresh, dazzling leg appearing from under his damask tunic. The same dazzling light suffuses the scene in which Laban, an old man with the air of a prophet, accompanied by a young man, Jacob (in whom we may recognize Tiepolo's self-portrait), in a crowd of bystanders, bends down towards Rachel to demand the idols. The play of reflected lights seems to have been studied from nature, with the rendering of the atmosphere as a major preoccupation. In the middle distance the figures have already lost substance and become paler and diaphanous, and here one can clearly see how much the landscape painters of the eighteenth century owe to Tiepolo, and to what extent he was a precursor of the modern *plein air* movement. The group of shepherds with oxen and sheep and the peasant woman with the babies on the left, are among the most luminous passages in the arcadian painting of the time.

After having frescoed the staircase and the splendid gallery, Tiepolo then decorated the third and last part of the former Patriarchate with the *Judgement of Solomon* (Pl. 10). The perspective problem was here a fairly difficult one, in view of the limited height of the room, but the artist solved it by using very moderately foreshortened figures, seen from below. This was probably the first time he represented so crowded an historical composition on a ceiling. Brilliantly observed details, such as the dwarf with the dog – a homage to Veronese – or that of the corpulent dignitary with the look of a Vitellius, again inspired by Veronese, or finally, the brutal soldier threatening to split in half, like a rabbit, the poor little baby he holds head downwards; these are passages of such exuberant vitality and of such fresh naturalness as eighteenth-century painting had never before seen.

When he had finished the frescoes in Udine, Tiepolo returned to Venice to his family. Since 1719, he had, in fact, been married to Cecilia Guardi, the sister of the painters Antonio and Francesco. Cecilia was seventeen at the time of the marriage, which was a happy one and blessed with nine children; in 1727, the third child, Domenico, was born, the most faithful and brilliant collaborator of his father, and in 1736, Lorenzo, who was also a painter, but of much less ability than his brother. It is pleasant to visualize the family life of Tiepolo in these early years as he himself represented his own studio in the small picture of *Alexander and Campaspe in the Studio of Apelles,* now in Montreal (Col. Pl. II). Apelles painting at the easel is certainly Tiepolo himself, Campaspe may be Cecilia Guardi, a little plump as she appears so many years later in the family picture by Lorenzo in the Rosebery Coll., and the little negro is the painter's servant, the faithful Ali. One of the canvases propped against the wall represents the *Brazen Serpent,* the other is a religious subject. Naturally, in the studio of Giambattista there was no perspective of an immense courtyard with a statue of Hercules . . . . but there was, certainly, the white pekinese, which we see in other pictures of this period. In this little picture, unemphatic, natural and truthful, the candid and spontaneous genius of Tiepolo is fully evident.

II

EARLY MATURITY:

TRAVELS IN LOMBARDY AND THE VENETO

1731–1740

WHEN, in 1731, Tiepolo was called to Milan to fresco the Archinto and Casati (Dugnani) Palaces, he was then 35 years old, but his art was still continually developing. It was in this decade, during the interval between his first frescoes and his last Milanese fresco – that in the Palazzo Clerici, executed in 1740 – that Giambattista finally achieved his classic style. It was during this period that he eliminated all trace of dark Seicento tonality and heaviness of colour, that he overcame that tendency towards a too nervous and agitated undulation in his line (which can still occasionally be seen at Udine), that he strove resolutely to achieve an equilibrium in his masses, a clarity of form resolved in complete harmony and full transparency of colour. The line is flowing, pure, and singing; the plasticity of his pictorial vision is blended softly with the atmosphere, the figures in the ceilings no longer weigh heavy, but float up there, ethereal, weightless, joyous, in an ideal perfection of beauty.

For all that he was assailed with commissions and overwhelmed with work, Tiepolo never rested upon his laurels. He never stayed still; for him, it was a continual struggle to improve and to renew his ideas which gave him no rest. He treated certain themes an infinity of times, without ever showing any sign of weariness, without ever repeating himself and with an inexhaustible variety of ever new images. He was helped in this by the range of his imagination, an imagination which daily invented new motives with that fresh spontaneity and that richness of inspiration which illumines the greatest musical geniuses. Like a music of colour and light, Tiepolo's visions take hold of us and exalt us. But the road by which Tiepolo reached such a supreme goal was long and arduous, even for an artist of his facility.

In the Palazzo Archinto he painted four ceilings, which were all destroyed during the last war, in 1943. In the principal saloon he painted a *Triumph of the Arts*; in the other rooms mythological scenes, the most successful of which was that of *Phaethon begging Apollo to allow him to drive the chariot of the Sun* (Pl. 12). Before beginning the fresco, Tiepolo tried out various solutions of the theme in drawings and sketches. Two of these must be considered as *modelli* which the painter submitted for the approval

Fig. 13. SOPHONISBA RECEIVING THE POISON FROM MASSINISSA.
Fresco, 1731. Milan, Palazzo Dugnani

Fig. 14. SAINT JOHN THE BAPTIST PREACHING. 1732–33.
Milan, Treccani Collection

Fig. 15. THE BATTLE OF VERCELLAE. About 1725–30.
New York, Camillo Castiglioni Collection

Fig. 16. THE DECOLLATION OF SAINT JOHN THE BAPTIST. 1732–33.
Stockholm, Museum

Fig. 17. THE LAST COMMUNION OF SAINT JEROME. About 1732–33. Stuttgart, Staatsgalerie

Fig. 18. THE DEATH OF SAINT JEROME. About 1732–33. Milan, Poldi-Pezzoli Museum

of the patron before starting on the work; one is now in the Bowes Museum at Barnard Castle, Durham, the other is in the Akademie in Vienna (Pl. 13). In the same year, 1731, when he had finished the frescoes in the Palazzo Archinto, the artist decorated the principal saloon of the Palazzo Dugnani (then Casati), depicting on the ceiling a great *Allegory of Magnanimity,* and on the walls three Roman histories, *Sophonisba receiving the poison sent by Massinissa* (Fig 13), the *Continence of Scipio* and *Scipio and the Slave.* It will not be difficult to perceive in this cycle of frescoes a further step towards the conquest of light, and a greater simplicity of pictorial language. He groups and moves his figures with the skill of a great theatrical producer – in the Baroque stage setting every character has its own illumination and significance – from those minor figures in the front plane, whose sole function is to give a sense of depth, to that of the warrior bearing the poison, huge in his shadowed mass, ineluctable as Fate, up to the protagonist, picked out in the full light, who, after reading the tragic message, now prepares herself to take the poison, amid the lamentations of the chorus. Theatre, if you like – but a painted theatre splendid with colour, magnetic and fascinating.

But it was theatre only when Tiepolo wanted it so. In the treatment of other subjects, and above all in religious pictures, his pathos is of an inward kind, controlled and profoundly spiritual. The religious feeling of the painter – and there can be no doubt about this – was sincere and instinctive. The grand gestures, when they occur, are the expression of pain, of tragedy, of martyrdom. With what sense of intimate religious poetry he treated, at this time, various sacred themes can be seen in the *Adoration of the Infant Jesus,* painted in the last months of 1732, when he had only just returned to Venice, for the Church of S. Giuliano, and now in the Sacristy of S. Mark's, or in the two canvases in the great hall of the Scuola di S. Rocco, of *Abraham visited by the Angels* and *Hagar and Ishmael* (Pls. 14, 15), or in the great altarpiece of the *Education of the Virgin* in the Chiesa della Fava (Pls. 16, 18). All are works of great verve, rich in their chiaroscuro, with clear echoes of Piazzetta, and yet, in a certain sense, less advanced than the frescoes already executed in Milan, from which we may infer that Tiepolo's major advances were made in his wall paintings.

In the autumn of the same year, 1732, he was at Bergamo where he frescoed four allegorical figures in the cupola of the Colleoni Chapel, and he returned there in the following autumn to paint in the chapel itself some scenes from the life of S. John the Baptist. For this also, as was his habit, he prepared *modelletti*; one for the *Preaching of the Baptist* is in the Treccani Coll. in Milan, and another for the *Decollation of the Baptist* is in the National Museum, Stockholm. These *modelletti* of the Bergamo period are distinguished by the granular nature of the paint (almost as if sandy) and by a bolder and more impetuous touch, which indicates approximately the masses of the light and shadow, as well as by an incisiveness in the drawing of the contours of the figures. If one thinks back to the sketches of the Udine period the progress is evident. It can also be seen in two other pictures, again of the same small size and pervaded with inimitable religious poetry – the *Last Communion of S. Jerome,* in the Staatsgalerie, Stuttgart, and the *Death of S. Jerome* in the Poldi-Pezzoli Museum, Milan. The preparation for the hermit's holy death is the theme of the first; death itself, rendered sweet by the presence of the angels who form a crown around the Saint, outstretched on the ground, is the subject of the other. Two moving incidents in a tender religious drama, rendered more intense by the sobriety of colour which plays in tones of silvery and leaden greys over a subtly varied underpainting (Figs. 14, 16-18). At about this time Tiepolo painted three big canvases, like a triptych, for the main saloon of the Villa Grimani-Valmarana at Noventa Padovana. They represent an episode from Roman history with a hunter and a horseman as the laterals. The centre is now in the Johnson Collection, Philadelphia, and the laterals in the M. Crespi Collection, Milan (Fig. 19).

To the Bergamo period may also be assigned the imposing altarpiece in the parish church of Rovetta sopra Bergamo, in which Tiepolo represented, in homage to the dedication of the church to All Saints, *The Virgin in Glory, adored by the Apostles and Saints* (Pls. 17, 19, 20). In this dazzling picture, saturated with colour, orchestrated in reds and yellows and shrill violets, but also subtly modified by the exact tonal values, Tiepolo eliminated all remaining traces of Piazzetta (which still appeared in the Venetian altarpieces mentioned earlier) and displays his powers as a colourist, among the greatest of his time. The brushwork is full, modelling the form with an almost sensual pleasure in the paint. The massive and solemn figure of S. Peter, brandishing his key, dominates the scene; behind him is S. Paul's aquiline profile, while nearby kneels S. John, Bishop of Bergamo – the three figures forming a compact group, a scenic effect of great force in the presentation of the stage crowded with other saints. This altarpiece is one of the major examples of Tiepolo as a colourist.

It also marks, in my opinion, a crucial point in his development. It was difficult to go beyond it, in the use of rich and saturated colour, and in his next major work, the *Road to Calvary* in S. Alvise, Venice (Fig. 20.), the exertions of the painter are evident, both in organizing the immensely crowded scene (flanked by two canvases of the *Flagellation* and the *Crowning with Thorns*), and in finding the exact colour relations for the triptych. Too bright colours were abandoned for a calmer, graver tone, as the theme required, but the power of imagery and the impetuous force of the handling are far greater. Tiepolo, as if moved to anguish by the sacred story, leaves on one side all search after classical, formal beauty, to concentrate solely on effects of the utmost dramatic pathos, in which are echoes of Titian and Rembrandt, especially in the *Calvary,* where a surging, inchoate crowd, driven by a gust of homicidal madness, hastens on the martyrdom of Christ. This is no variation on a set theme, for the artist's vision is entirely new in the iconography of the subject, from the Christ who falls broken beneath the weight of the Cross, to the Veronica gazing at the Holy Face imprinted on her cloth. The two thieves, the good one who halts to look pityingly at the Saviour, the bad one, unmoved, who goes on his way – figures of great pictorial power – have no precedent of such psychological penetration in the painting of the time.

Having abandoned for this great sacred theme all research into form in the classical sense, Tiepolo resumed, in the years towards 1740, his efforts to find a new concept of the human figure. In the two immense canvases of Verolanuova, of the *Gathering of the Manna* (Pls. 21-23) and the *Sacrifice of Melchisedek* (Fig. 21), he had already created passages of classic beauty and elegance, of fresh and serene luminosity, as of a Raphael or a Poussin revived, in which were set out for the first time some new ideals of Tiepolesque beauty. These ideals took more concrete form in the three canvases formerly in the Villa Girola on Lake Como, which later passed to Artaria in Vienna, and of which the *Triumph of Amphitrite* (Pl. 28) is now in Dresden. Both in these and in the *Danaë* in the Stockholm University Museum (Col. Pl. IV), painted just before 1736 for Count Tessin, the Swedish Minister in Venice, Tiepolo showed that he had no more doubts (such as had appeared earlier in Udine and elsewhere) about his own ideal of female beauty. It is a radiant beauty, with rounded limbs, inspired by the Venuses of Titian and Veronese, which must have been the incarnation of contemporary Italian ideals of beauty. That Tiepolo drew his inspiration from one of his models, a certain Cristina, daughter of a gondolier, is an oft-repeated but misleading flight of the imagination of the Venetian historian Urbani de Gheltof; but what is clear is that even if the model were not this Cristina, some very lovely woman must have posed for him.

It may be assumed that Tiepolo worked on several things at the same time, especially if one considers his vast production in mural painting, for the execution of which he had to wait for favourable weather. Thus, there must have been intervals in the course of the work on the ceiling of *S. Dominic instituting the Rosary* (Col. Pl. III) in the Gesuati, on which he had been working since May, 1737, but which was not finished before October, 1739. In this ceiling, which is very high up, Tiepolo adopted a perspective strongly foreshortened from below and used – as had, incidentally, Veronese, though with less emphasis – various architectural elements, on which he disposed his figures in order to achieve a greater sense of depth. First comes the personification of the Albigensian heresy, crushed by the Saint, which flings itself – like the devil in the staircase at Udine – out of the composition; then on the cornice, two warriors with halberds; next, on the steep staircase, the group of the faithful among whom is a bishop in an ample cope of gold brocade; finally, the Saint himself, high up on the top steps, near the balustrade. With such a play of successively receding planes the painter gives an hallucinating and vertiginous illusion of space.

Tiepolo's activity in the fourth decade of the century closes with a major work, which marks a new stage in the conquest of the painting of skies – namely, the ceiling of the Palazzo Clerici in Milan (Pls. 25–27). His success was such that it was hardly finished when an anonymous Milanese poet extolled the masterpiece in a series of poems dedicated *'al merito singolarissimo'* of the artist, whom he calls by the title of *'imitatore di Paolo Veronese',* with the intention of thus exalting him to the same level as one of the greatest glories of Italian painting. The rich, gallant and prodigal commissioner, the Marchese Giorgio Clerici, general of the Empress Maria Teresa, could well afford to be satisfied too, for with this work he endowed Milan with one of the most fascinating pictorial creations of the century. Tiepolo here introduced a new compositional principle, foreshadowed in the Palazzo Sandi, which may be described as centrifugal, and which was crucial for his future development, from Würzburg to Madrid; he freed the central field from all dense masses and pushed groups of figures along the edges of the ceiling, thus achieving a much more effective plasticity in the figures placed almost on the walls, and, by contrast, a more luminous brilliance and lightness in the distant figures. In the distance, almost in the middle of the sky, appears, with the emerging chariot of Apollo, the Sun which lights the universe, and round him the deities of Olympus and creatures of the earth come to life. It is a lively and joyous crowd, personifications of the rivers and the winds, nymphs and sirens, nereids and tritons, groups of courtiers and dwarfs, negroes and orientals with camels, elephants and crocodiles symbolizing the four quarters of the earth. It is a welter of Baroque fantasy. But what stupendous equilibrium is in the seeming disorder of the figures ! It is the exaltation of life by a society which had fashioned this life above all into a spectacular and sensual vision of beauty, in a feast of colour, and there is but one single, thoughtful shadow in this scintillating ceiling: the allegory of Beauty ravished by Time, in the guise of Venus and Saturn – the only reminder of tomorrow.

Fig. 19. A SCENE FROM ROMAN HISTORY. About 1730–35. Philadelphia, John G. Johnson Collection
(the two laterals in the M. Crespi Collection, Milan)

Fig. 20. THE ROAD TO CALVARY; THE FLAGELLATION; THE CROWNING WITH THORNS. About 1738–40. Venice, Chiesa di S. Alvise

Fig. 23. THE MIRACLE OF THE HOLY HOUSE OF LORETO.
Ceiling fresco, 1743, in the Chiesa degli Scalzi, Venice,
destroyed in 1915

Fig. 22. MADONNA DEL CARMELO. Ceiling canvas, 1740.
Venice, Scuola dei Carmini

Fig. 21. THE SACRIFICE OF MELCHISEDEK. About 1735–40.
Verolanuova, Parish Church

III

FULL MATURITY:

THE GREAT DECORATIVE CYCLES IN VENICE

1741 – 1750

A PERIOD of intensely hard work lay before Tiepolo in the fifth decade of the century. Not yet able to call on the help of his two sons (Domenico began to be useful to his father only towards the second half of the decade; Lorenzo at least another five years later), he had to carry alone the exceptional weight of the innumerable commissions which crowded upon him. He produced a number of altarpieces, frescoed the ceilings of churches, painted on canvas or in fresco in the most splendid Venetian palaces. The most illustrious families of the Republic sought eagerly to have paintings or a room decorated by him – for example, the Mocenigo, the Corner, the Pisani, the Barbaro, the Donà dalle Rose, the Barbarigo-Rezzonico, the Labia families. This was the decade of the artist's unchallenged mastery, for he had already reached this eminence through widely celebrated works such as the ceiling of the Palazzo Clerici in Milan. Secure in the brilliance of his talent, Tiepolo unhesitatingly undertook any and every decorative theme, no matter how complex; rather did he seem to enjoy developing such themes in the most grandiose way. Thus, in sacred subjects, the fresco in the church of the Scalzi and the one in the church of the Pietà surpassed that in the Gesuati; thus the ceilings at Würzburg and then those in Madrid mark the final triumphs of his art. This does not mean, of course, that the early works are inferior to those of his maturity. The Udine frescoes, for example, or the great canvas of the *Calvary* in S. Alvise, are masterpieces in their own right, merely different from the later ones.

In this period one can see the classical ideas becoming fixed, a positive desire for decorative balance and, in the quality of his paint, a greater fusion and transparency.

Before completing the frescoes in the Palazzo Clerici in Milan, Tiepolo had been commissioned by the Council of the Scuola del Carmine in Venice (who, in their deliberations on the 21st December, 1739, had referred to him as 'the most celebrated of the virtuosi') to decorate the ceiling of their Assembly Room. In the following January, Tiepolo accepted their terms and proposed the various subjects, which were to be painted on canvas, and to have in the centre 'a Madonna descending from Heaven, holding in her hand a holy scapular which she proffers to S. Simon Stock', and in the other compartments were to be groups of two or three virtues. The painter worked on these canvases at various times between 1740 and 1743, and when the series was finished, such was the applause that he was elected a member of the confraternity. The *Virgin with the Scapular* is, in fact, one of the most noble expressions of Venetian painting since the days of Titian and Veronese, but here, clearly, a completely different sensibility and stylistic intention is at work; the forms are bathed in a more atmospheric light, the figures float weightlessly. A flickering silvery light plays over everything, the flimsy veils flutter in the eddies created by the beating of the angels' wings, there is a paean of white, Tiepolo's favourite colour (Fig. 22)

In these same years – 1743-44 – Tiepolo reached a further stage of his pictorial evolution with the immense ceiling of the church of the Scalzi, where he frescoed the *Miracle of the Holy House of Loreto.* The architecture of the ceiling opens (or rather, opened, since it was destroyed in 1915) in a large shaped oval of sky, in which appears, above the little house of Nazareth, the white figure of the Virgin with the Child, a tiny figure surrounded by an immense celestial crowd, yet nevertheless so powerful a fulcrum that on it is centred the spellbound attention of the spectator, maybe because on her converge (or from her emanate) the leading lines of the composition, or because around her there is a huge empty zone of sky, which here grows in mysterious luminosity. This work in the church of the Scalzi was the religious masterpiece of these years, his major religious fresco (Fig. 23). Later, he was to paint other Heavens in churches, such as the one in the Purità in Udine, or in the Pietà in Venice, but they were lesser works. His major works in fresco were in future to be devoted almost exclusively to secular subjects.

In this decade, so far as we know, the artist left Venice only once, and this was to decorate the Villa Cordellina, at Montecchio Maggiore near Vicenza, with frescoes which still survive, though they are in rather poor state. For these, as usual, he supplied *modelletti,* one of which, of the *Continence of Scipio* (Pl. 29), is now in the Museum at Stockholm, the other, of the *Family of Darius,* is in the Crespi Collection in Milan. From Montecchio Tiepolo wrote to Count Algarotti, his friend and patron, on the 26th October, 1743, a letter which is interesting because it gives an insight into his character and into his working methods. Firstly, he states that the ceiling (now in the Museum in Vicenza) was well advanced, and that he would have carried it even further had the 'uncertain weather' permitted. Evidently Tiepolo liked to work in fresco only in fine, dry weather, either to be able to gauge the colour better, or else because the painting dried at once, and he could then work much faster. 'By now,' he adds, 'I have already finished eight grisailles and I have almost half finished the ceiling, which I flatter myself – indeed, I am sure – I shall finish by the 10th or the 12th of next month.' He had, then, a pre-arranged and very precise programme, and reckoned on painting a ceiling of about eleven metres by six in less than a month. But this time, already short in itself, was rendered even shorter, the painter lamented, by the distractions caused by the residents of the Villa. 'Here I am,' the letter continues, 'and I can do nothing because there are too many visitors,' clear proof that the guests in the Villa disturbed him by their presence and their chattering. 'I swear that I should much prefer,' the letter ends, 'one day in your company talking of painting, than all the amusements in this villa, which, believe me, are not a few. Bear in mind to do at least something yourself, the moment your own sublime talent suggests it to you.' These lines disclose not only Tiepolo's passion for painting, which he puts before any amusement, but also his reluctance to be idle for a single hour, lamenting the time lost at the villa on account of the guests, and begging Count Algarotti, whose talent he describes as sublime, to do some work himself. We can forget about Algarotti's 'talent', of which only a few pitiful examples are known. What is certain is that the contact with this man of the world – a well-read essayist, an amateur painter, an art dealer and a man of considerable brilliance – played its part in Giambattista's artistic development. The friendship between them was of long standing, and mutually profitable, since the Count made use of Tiepolo as a connoisseur of painting and had the benefit of his judgement, above all on the works of art which he bought on behalf of Augustus III of Saxony, and for his part, Count Algarotti spread through all the courts of Europe and the world of art the fame of the Venetian painter, whose works yearly became more sought after.

It was, in fact, in 1743 that Algarotti ordered from Tiepolo, for the Saxon Minister, a *Banquet of Antony and Cleopatra* painted with extreme care and refinement, which later passed to the Hermitage, and from there to the National Gallery in Melbourne (Fig. 28). This is a phase of some delicacy in the art of the master, who seems to submit to Algarotti's suggestions in his search for cosmopolitan elegance, a little Frenchified, and of which there will still be lively reflections in the future, in works of a purely decorative type, of refined elegance and consummate bravura, as for example in the four scenes of *Rinaldo and Armida* (Pls. 69 and 72) now in the Art Institute in Chicago, and in the *Finding of Moses* (Pls. 70, 71) in Edinburgh, all of a later period.

The elegant and slightly superficial style of these secular paintings was tempered, as if by an urge to greater sincerity to himself, by other creations of greater artistic content and more profound feeling. Among these are the various canvases on the theme of the Passion which Tiepolo must have executed between 1745 and 1750 and which it is possible – conjecturally and at least in part – to reconstruct as a series. These are the *Agony in the Garden* and the *Crowning with Thorns* (Pls. 30-33) in the Kunsthalle, Hamburg, the *Last Supper* in the Louvre and the *Crucifixion* in St. Louis (Figs. 24, 25); canvases of the same size and identical style, which originally must have been together. Deeply felt, they were conceived at a time when the artist's mind was dominated by the pathos of the Christian drama. Of the first two, the late Professor Lorenzetti wrote, 'In both the canvases the light is the guiding principle; in the *Crowning with*

21

Thorns it is the light of the full mid-day sun which invests and defines every form, every single figure in the tumultuous crowd – types of old orientals which Rembrandt's etchings might have suggested to the painter; the illumination of a lightning flash in the *Agony in the Garden,* which suddenly rends the darkness of the night, and lights with ghostly effect the crowd which stops, awestruck, hesitant, before the portentous vision'.

In this decade the moments were rare in which the painter could withdraw into himself to create works of such powerful religous emotion, overwhelmed as he was by the commissions for secular decorations for palaces in Venice itself, which were mainly allegories or else themes from mythology or ancient history.

Thus he painted for the Palazzo Barbaro a large canvas for the ceiling with an *Apotheosis of Francesco Barbaro,* now in the Metropolitan Museum of Art, New York, as well as four oval overdoors, which today are dispersed – the *Offering of Gifts to Cleopatra,* signed, in the Colonna Coll., Turin; *Timoclea and the Captain* in the National Gallery, Washington; *Tarquin and Lucretia* in the Haberstock Coll., Berlin; and the *Betrothal* in the Museum at Copenhagen. They are pictures of the most subtle decorative taste, and very solidly painted, when one remembers that they were to fill a purely decorative function. From this same time must also date the splendid *Marriage Allegory of the Cornaro Family,* painted for the Palazzo Corner-Mocenigo and now in the Contini Coll. in Florence; in it Tiepolo expresses ideals of beauty which Veronese himself, had he returned to life, would not have hesitated to accept as his own, transmuted by two centuries of pictorial experience. And as in the *Apotheosis of Francesco Barbaro* the bearded old man is certainly a portrait of the protagonist, so here the young man leaning towards his wife must also undoubtedly be a portrait (Figs. 26, 27).

Very few portraits by Tiepolo survive, although from his earliest years he had a distinct feeling for character, as may be seen from his numerous self-portraits, from the Udine period onwards. Da Canal records that he had painted several portraits in the Casa Cornaro, all now lost, and he painted very few in the following years, being always occupied with large schemes of decoration. But many superb portraits are to be found in his frescoes, and it suffices to mention those at Würzburg, which will be discussed later. As independent works on canvas, two male portraits only have survived: the half-length of Antonio Riccobono, in the Accademia dei Concordi at Rovigo (Pls. 34 and 36) and the full length of the Procurator Giovanni Querini, in the Galleria Querini-Stampalia in Venice (Pls. 35 and 37). The first is an imaginary portrait, drawn perhaps from some old iconographical record, or more probably based on a man of imposing and severe aspect who served as a model for Riccobono, who lived two centuries earlier. But what a new pose (almost Rembrandtesque) in the figure; how the figure is made to stand out against the background, sharply divided into two fields by the streak of light; what an intense pulsation of life in the noble, powerful head of the

Fig. 24. THE LAST SUPPER. About 1745–50. Paris, Louvre

Fig. 25. THE CRUCIFIXION. About 1745–50. St. Louis, Museum

Fig. 26. MARRIAGE ALLEGORY OF THE CORNARO FAMILY.
About 1745–50.
Florence, Count Contini Bonacossi Collection

Fig. 27. APOTHEOSIS OF FRANCESCO BARBARO. Ceiling from the Palazzo Barbaro, Venice, about 1745–50.
New York, Metropolitan Museum

Fig. 28. THE BANQUET OF CLEOPATRA. Shortly after 1744. Melbourne, National Gallery of Victoria

Fig. 29. CONSILIUM IN ARENA. 1748–50. Udine, Museo Civico

Fig. 30. THE MEETING OF ANTONY AND CLEOPATRA. About 1747. Paris, E. de Rothschild Collection

Fig. 31. THE BANQUET OF CLEOPATRA. About 1747. London, Alexander Collection

old man ! The rapid movement with which he turns suddenly towards the hypothetical interlocutor has that instantaneous quality of unpremeditated naturalness which Tiepolo could, on occasion, catch so well. On the other hand, an entirely different spirit informs the portrait of the Procurator Querini, which is a kind of Symphony in Red, composed of the fiery colour of the robe, of the stole and of the velvet on the small table. The monumental figure stands in a vista of Palladian architecture seen from below (the portrait was evidently designed to be hung high up) which accentuates the feeling of spatial depth in measured, rhythmical distances. But it is the new and spiritual attitude pervading this unique example of the artist's psychological insight which is important. This face, pallid as wax, with a keen and pungent expression, far from being an idealization, seizes the character almost to the point of satire. The subtle vein of humour which ran hidden in Tiepolo here spurted out in this amazing creation. This vein was to be taken up and developed by Domenico in some of the most significant passages of satirical painting in the eighteenth century.

This work makes one regret all the more that Tiepolo did not more often practise portraiture, in which he would certainly have been able to offer an unparalleled gallery of his contemporaries. He had a subtly humorous gift of observation of which there remain vivid traces in so many of his caricature drawings (Pls. 40 and 41), in which the comic side of humanity is laid bare. At odd moments where floated up in him that witty spirit, bantering and sharp, yet without malice – natural to the Venetian – of which the comedies of Carlo Goldoni are the unsurpassed literary monument. But in Tiepolo's own day the idea of the classical Grand Manner was dominant and he persevered in it, perhaps because of the continual promptings of Algarotti. The scenes of popular life, parallel to the world of Goldoni's satires, will, in the course of time, become the particular domain of his son Domenico.

That the classic world dominated Tiepolo's mind may be seen in the grandiose decorations in the central saloon of the Palazzo Labia (Pls. 46-49). With the help of Mengozzi-Colonna for the perspective parts, Tiepolo here created one of the most beautiful examples of pictorial illusionism ever painted. The room is nearly square, very high and light; in the ceiling is *Genius on Pegasus putting Time to Flight*; on the walls, on the one side the *Meeting of Antony and Cleopatra* and on the other the *Banquet of Cleopatra,* and groups of secondary figures or glimpses of long perspectives can be seen between the imitation, painted columns. Tiepolo must have striven his utmost to achieve the maximum of clarity and lucidity of form in this complex. In the drawing there is absolute precision, almost a tautness in the tension of pure line. The colour is of a vivid transparency, luminous even in the shadows, as if of a vitreous paste. There is an absolute supremacy over every element of pictorial art, and the knowledge of human form, in relation to the perspective, seems as if intuitive and completely effortless.

The theme of Antony and Cleopatra lent itself to Tiepolo's imagination, as is evident from the *Banquet* already mentioned, painted for the Saxon Minister and now in Melbourne. But at about the same time as the frescoes in the Palazzo Labia, many other paintings must have originated which can be linked to them, such, for example, as the *Meeting of Antony and Cleopatra* in the National Gallery, Edinburgh, to which the pendant is perhaps the *Banquet* in the Museum in Stockholm; and again, the *Meeting* in the Rothschild Coll. in Paris goes with the *Banquet* in the Alexander Coll. in London. It is probable, in fact, that the painter supplied the two subjects in pairs (Figs. 30-33).

Also in this period, between 1745 and 1750, Tiepolo executed two pictures in the purest classical vein – a secular one for the Ducal Palace in Venice, and a religious one for the church of S. Agata at Lendinara. The former is the allegory of *Neptune offering to Venice the Riches of the Sea* (Pls. 42-44), the latter is the *Martyrdom of S. Agatha* now in the Museum at Berlin (Pl. 51, Col. Pl. V). The first is an exaltation of the greatness of the Republic (a greatness which was to end miserably in another half-century), the second is one of the most touching religious works ever created by the artist. The theme of the martyrdom of the Saint, whose breast has been cut off by the executioner, had already been treated by the artist in an altarpiece in the Santo in Padua. Here he takes it up again, but with a much more intense dramatic feeling, with a stricken expression in the emaciated face of the Saint, white as death, which will not again be found except perhaps in certain passages of the Este altarpiece. A moving painting, shot through with a spasm of suffering so intensely human, that it enables us to share a vision of delirious agony in which the tragic theme is overwhelmed by divine ecstasy.

A picture unique in Tiepolo's *œuvre,* commemorating an historical event, was painted at the end of the decade for Count Montegnacco of Udine. Wishing to record the Council of the Order of Malta, which, meeting in 1748, admitted him and his friend Count Florio to its ranks, he commissioned the artist to paint the scene, prescribing the most minute details of the event. This is the *Consilium in Arena* in the Museum at Udine (Fig. 29), the keystone for the understanding of one of the least obvious aspects of Tiepolo as an illustrator, or what would nowadays be called a documentary painter. Above all, it is a keystone for understanding the point of departure of the art of his son Domenico, who was, in fact, a humorous and pungent illustrator of the life of his times, as may be seen in the frescoes in the *Foresteria* of the Villa Valmarana, the scenes of the 'New World', formerly in the Villa de Zanigo and now in the Ca' Rezzonico, and, finally, in the satirical drawings already mentioned. Now, it is not too rash to suggest that Domenico collaborated in this painting. He was then twenty-two and had already given proofs of his ability in the *Stations of the Cross* executed a few years earlier for the church of the Frari. Such collaboration is extremely difficult to distinguish in these years when Domenico sought to identify himself with his father.

IV

THE YEARS IN WÜRZBURG

12th December, 1750 to 8th November, 1753

FROM the summer of 1750, Tiepolo had been commissioned to go to the capital of Franconia in order to fresco the Dining Room (or Kaisersaal) of the new Residenz, which was being completed according to the plans of the Bohemian architect Balthasar Neumann. The negotiations were conducted in Venice by the German banker Mehling, agent of the Prince-Bishop, Carl Philip von Greiffenklau; and they were not easy. Finally, on the 12th October, Tiepolo accepted the munificent terms offered him, and two months later arrived in Würzburg, where he was received with great honour, with his two sons, Domenico, aged twenty-three, and Lorenzo, barely fourteen. He immediately set to work in close collaboration with the exquisite Venetian stuccoist and ornamentalist Felice Bossi, in order to establish the programme of the plastic and pictorial decoration of the saloon. In April, 1751, Tiepolo was able to show the Prince the sketches for the ceiling, which was uncovered on the 8th July following. The two historical scenes on the walls (one of which is signed and dated 1752) were painted soon after and finished in July of that year, 1752. The room was not yet completely finished when the Prince, delighted with Tiepolo's work, besought him to fresco the staircase as well, and by April of 1752 he approved the sketches of the painter (a large *modello* for the staircase has recently been discovered in London: Fig. 35) and settled with him a contract which was to remunerate him even more magnificently than for the Kaisersaal (Pl. 54). The admirable ceiling was painted in the space of little over a year, with long interruptions caused, necessarily, by the winter weather. On the 8th November, 1753, Tiepolo left the city for home.

In the three years of his stay in Würzburg, Tiepolo accomplished two pictorial schemes which are among the greatest creations of figurative art; a gift of his genius to the episcopal city and to Germany, which long saw in these paintings an incomparable example of artistic perfection. In fact, Tiepolo's influence on the monumental painting of Catholic Germany was immense, but it is also indubitable that, living in a new artistic ambience, and in contact with men of great culture, Tiepolo himself was stimulated by new ideas which excited his eager artistic spirit.

The frescoes in the Kaisersaal were to glorify some episodes in the life of the Emperor Frederic Barbarossa, by whom the Bishop of Würzburg was invested in 1168. On the

25

ceiling Tiepolo painted *Apollo conducting Barbarossa's bride, Beatrice of Burgundy* (Pls. 56, 64-66). The vast celestial space is more than half occupied by the dominant pictorial motive of the chariot of Apollo, drawn by the surging quadriga of white horses. In the chariot is seated, with her maid of honour and surrounded by putti and genii, the radiant bride, whom Apollo, high above the group, with the sweeping gesture of a *chef d'orchestre,* presents to Barbarossa. The Emperor awaits her on the high steps of the throne, his head crowned with laurels; over him floats Glory with a flaming torch, while surrounding him below are dignitaries of state, courtiers, warriors, symbolical figures. Of the many ceilings which Tiepolo had painted up to that time, this one excelled them all by the complexity, and yet clarity of the invention, by the harmonious massing and by the joyousness of the colour. The motive of the horse seen foreshortened from below, already indicated in embryo in the ceilings of the Sandi, Clerici and Labia palaces, here emerges as fundamentally important to the figurative ensemble, bringing to mind all the horses launched across the skies by Baroque painters, from Guercino to Reni, from Giordano to Solimena, and one can find nothing which can be compared with this divine quadriga rearing weightlessly amid the clouds, in the immensity of an atmosphere suffused by air and sunlight, in which the fanfares of colour, as in a brilliant symphony, sound the most radiant and joyous anthems. The sketch for this ceiling is in Stuttgart (Fig. 36).

The artist's imagination was allowed less freedom in the two frescoes on the walls, where he had to represent two scenes from German mediaeval history, which, however, given the inadequate knowledge of the iconography of that period, Tiepolo, with artistic licence, transferred into the costumes of the Italian sixteenth century, interpreting them in the style of Veronese. The two representations, one of the *Marriage of Barbarossa* (Colour Pl. VII), the other of the *Investiture of Bishop Harold* (Pl. 67), are imagined as taking place at the front of a stage, disclosed behind the heavy curtains of gilded stucco, lifted up by angels. In neither fresco is there much depth of perspective, because their high siting did not allow the artist to place the figures of the foreground too far behind the picture plane, but passages of the highest quality compensate for the restrictions — here and there obvious — imposed by the theme of these two compositions. Besides the drawings, Tiepolo made *modelletti* for all these works, but some of these *modelletti* appear to be records of the frescoes themselves, rather than sketches or studies for them. The Boston sketch of the *Marriage of Barbarossa* (Fig. 34) is clearly a study for the fresco, but the London one may perhaps be such a record. Round the fresco in the ceiling, between Bossi's rococo cartouches of stucco, which reveal glimpses of the sky, Tiepolo painted pagan deities and flying putti, while in the pendentives and lunettes of the vault he painted Christian virtues, figures in antique or Renaissance costume, knights, pages, soldiers, with a purely decorative

Fig. 32. THE BANQUET OF CLEOPATRA. About 1745–50.
Stockholm, University Museum

Fig. 33. THE MEETING OF ANTONY AND CLEOPATRA.
About 1745–50. Edinburgh, National Gallery of Scotland

Fig. 34. THE MARRIAGE OF BARBAROSSA. 1751–52.
Sketch for the fresco at Würzburg.
Boston, Isabella Stewart Gardner Museum

Fig. 35. OLYMPUS, THE QUARTERS OF THE GLOBE,
AND OTHER ALLEGORIES. 1752. Sketch for the fresco at Würzburg.
London, formerly Hendon Hall Hotel

Fig. 36. APOLLO CONDUCTING BEATRICE OF BURGUNDY TO BARBAROSSA. 1751. Sketch for the fresco at Würzburg.
Stuttgart, Staatsgalerie

Fig. 37. RINALDO IN THE GARDEN OF ARMIDA. About 1755–60. Berlin, Gallery

intention, in which the collaboration of his son Domenico is clear. Domenico himself was also entrusted with the task of supplying four overdoors for the room. This whole room (Pl. 54), in the whiteness of the stucco touched with gold, in the shimmering richness of the colour, in the ethereal lightness of the ensemble, stands out as one of the most fascinating decorative schemes of the age.

A still larger task – indeed, the greatest which Tiepolo had so far attempted – awaited him in the ceiling over the Grand Staircase, where he had to depict Olympus (the ceiling is thirty metres by eighteen; Pls. 57–63 and 68). In the design of this immense apotheosis, Tiepolo developed ideas of composition which he had already in part used in the Palazzo Clerici in Milan, and gave definitive form to a pictorial idea which, in the Royal Palace in Madrid, will be used in a similar way. The task was to take the four parts of the known world and to magnify them into a kind of pagan and Catholic cosmorama, and above the continents there was to be the whole emporium of mythological and allegorical personifications which symbolized, and exalted, the humanistic aspirations of the eighteenth century. In the variety of its themes, this ceiling may almost be considered as an iconographical encyclopaedia of the Age of Enlightenment. In the centre of the sky, Apollo with the pagan deities and various allegorical figures pays homage to the Prince-Bishop von Greiffenklau, whose portrait, supported by putti and genii, holds the stage above the figure symbolizing Europe. This latter is personified by a richly clad woman, seated on a throne with her hand on the symbolic bull, and before whom bow the Sciences and the Arts. Various personages of the Court of Würzburg are arranged in ordered groups on the lower end of the ceiling, and the visitor climbing the stairs of the vast hall is immediately confronted with this impressive sight. Above the cornice of the exquisite architecture, with its rhythmic intervals of fluted pilasters, the fresco occupies the gently curved ceiling and the painted figures are placed above a second cornice, with figures in stucco at the angles which make the optical illusion even more hallucinating, so that one has difficulty in distinguishing between the real and painted elements.

In the foreground, in the centre of the principal side, comfortably seated on a cannon and near to a magnificent greyhound, is the architect of the palace, Balthasar Neumann, in a white peruke and in his uniform as a Colonel of Artillery. Behind him is the majestic figure of a young man in a cloak who may be either the German sculptor Auwera or the administrator of the palace. A charming little orchestra provides a subdued link between these persons and the group around Europe – an orchestra which recalls those by Veronese, but is more varied and animated (and what more natural than that they should be playing a concerto by Vivaldi !). In the left hand corner, over the shell cartouche with the two stucco nudes, appears Tiepolo's self-portrait and that of Domenico (Col. Pl. I), and near to them another person with ruddy face and shining nose, probably one of his collaborators, perhaps Urlaub or Roth. Above the cornice on the remaining three sides of the ceiling are crowded the representations of Asia, Africa and America, with all the iconographical congeries of the then known universe – a review of the human races (Col. Pl. VI), of costumes, fauna and flora.

This pictorial complex (notwithstanding the damages occasioned by time) is exhilarating and joyous in colour, instinct with life. The multi-coloured throng confronts us behind the aereal stage-setting of the staircase, deceiving our eyes with a magic world. The figures are grouped in harmonious masses, with rhythmical links between them, or daring twisted poses, forming a succession of episodes of spectacular inventiveness. Each element in the composition, however, has its gemlike relief made more prominent by the purity of the colour, rich in subtle juxtapositions, tying the effects of the maximum luminosity to the system of contrasts between warm and cold colours, between bright and dull ones. Above all, the painter is careful to keep light and transparent, even in the darkest passages, his areas of shadow, where the colour retains its fundamental value and all its intensity, so that one notices in the fresco no heavy or dark zones, but only soft and all-pervading light over the intricate play of forms. This transparency, which takes away all feeling of heaviness from the figures, is accentuated in the vast sky, where, in a blaze of light, through a veil of atmosphere, which shades into the distance through all the colours of the rainbow, the bodies become more ethereal and merge into the infinite.

This ceiling is one of the highest realizations of the genius of Tiepolo, whose maturity burgeons as in a perpetual spring, and ripens as in an endless summer. His high summer is long, and will last for many years; his creative vein is inexhaustible. In the three years of his stay in Germany, Giambattista also found the time to paint numerous works on canvas during the months when fresco-painting was impossible. For the Residenz, Tiepolo executed two paintings of episodes taken from the Gerusalemme Liberata, representing *Rinaldo in the garden of Armida* and *Rinaldo abandoning Armida,* now in the Alte Pinakothek, Munich, – motives which will be taken up again and developed in the Villa Valmarana frescoes of a few years later. Linked to the Munich pictures, Giambattista also painted two delicious little canvases, one in the Berlin Museum and the other in the Cailleux Collection in Paris, both spirited and scintillating in handling (Figs. 37 and 38). At this period Tiepolo also painted two delightful canvases, *Armida crowning the sleeping Rinaldo with flowers* and *Armida and Rinaldo with a mirror,* now in a private collection in New York (Fig. 39). For the Court Chapel of the Residenz itself, he painted two large altarpieces, both dated 1752, of the *Fall of the Rebel Angels* and the *Assumption.*

He also worked outside Würzburg. For example, he painted for the church of the Benedictines of Schwarzach (both church and convent, built by Neumann, were

Fig. 38. RINALDO ABANDONS ARMIDA. About 1755–60. Paris, Cailleux Collection

Fig. 39. ARMIDA CROWNING THE SLEEPING RINALDO WITH FLOWERS; ARMIDA AND RINALDO WITH A MIRROR.
About 1750–55. New York, Private Collection

Fig. 40. THE ADORATION OF THE MAGI. About 1753.
New York, Metropolitan Museum

Fig. 41. THE DEATH OF HYACINTH. About 1752–53.
Lugano, Thyssen Collection

Fig. 42. RECEPTION OF THE EMPEROR HENRY III AT THE VILLA CONTARINI. Fresco, 1755–56. Paris, Musée Jacquemart-André

Fig. 43. THE TRIUMPH OF FAITH. Ceiling fresco, 1754–55.
Venice, Chiesa della Pietà

Fig. 44. APOTHEOSIS OF THE SODERINI FAMILY. Ceiling fresco, about 1754.
Formerly in the Villa Soderini-Berti at Nervesa .destroyed in 1917

Fig. 45. Giandomenico Tiepolo: THE CHARLATAN. Fresco, 1757. Vicenza, Villa Valmarana

Fig. 46. Giandomenico Tiepolo: THE DIORAMA. Fresco, 1757. Vicenza, Villa Valmarana

demolished at the beginning of the nineteenth century) the altarpiece of the *Adoration of the Magi* (Pls. 50, 52-53), now in the Alte Pinakothek in Munich, which is among his finest religious works. The artist has been able to invest every single figure with almost the same intensity of human love and magic radiance of colour, and the group of the Virgin and Child stands out in a blaze of brilliant sunlight. The same theme reappears in the small picture in the Metropolitan Museum, New York, which has been thought to be the preparatory sketch for the Schwarzach altarpiece, but the many differences in the composition and the more nervous quality in the drawing make one believe that the small picture must have been executed at a slightly later date (Fig. 40).

To this period also belongs the *Death of Hyacinth* formerly in Schloss Bückeburg in Germany, and now in the Thyssen Coll. in Lugano, painted in a pellucid freshness of colour, and for which there exist numerous preparatory drawings, which prove how much study the artist put into the gestatory period of his creations (Fig. 41).

Several other paintings, and, of course, drawings, done at Würzburg, were assigned to Tiepolo by his biographers, but in part these belong to Domenico, in part they are works of his school. A group of pupils remained, in fact, in the city, and continued the teachings of the master: we know that, in addition to Urlaub, there was Lucas Anton Flachner, who distinguished himself also as a Tiepolo copyist. The orbit of the Venetian's activity was not limited to Würzburg or to Franconia, but spread over the whole of Southern Germany, and particularly to Austria, where the Tiepolesque style – in the widest meaning of the word – achieved an imaginative and original development.

V

THE LAST DECADE

OF ACTIVITY IN VENICE AND THE VENETO

1753 – 1762

LADEN with the honours of Würzburg, where he had been welcomed, acclaimed and rewarded in a princely manner, Tiepolo returned to Venice with a wealth of precious experience. Contact with artists of the first rank, such as the great architect Neumann, the company of men with new ideas, and equally, the different air of the artistic and cultural atmosphere which he breathed for three years together, certainly had the effect of stimulating his pictorial inventiveness, and certainly influenced the evolution of his style, which takes on, in many of his works – and especially in the frescoes in the Villa Valmarana – a subtly fashionable, and, it may be said, a more French, flavour. But it was a passing phase. Tiepolo's art could not for long be subject to outside influence, since it was entirely self-sufficient and capable of spontaneous renewal. The artist, however, must have been aware that at Würzburg he had given of his very best, whether for the sake of raising high the banner of Venetian painting outside the confines of his own country, or because he had been stimulated by the *milieu* and by the Prince-Bishop, himself a great lover of painting and, in particular, a great admirer of Tiepolo. Certainly, he must have been conscious of having left an imperishable masterpiece on the other side of the Alps.

But he allowed himself little rest on his laurels, since, on the 12th June of the following year he began the ceiling of the Pietà, which 'was made visible', as is recorded by Pietro Gradenigo, on the 12th August 1755. In the central oval he represented the *Triumph of Faith,* the *modelletto* for which is in the Rosebery Coll. in London. The church of the Pietà was connected with the Istituto degli Esposti, one of the most famous musical schools in Venice on account of performances given by the foundling girls cared for there, and it would seem that those songs and that music re-echoed through the mind of the artist when he was thinking out the composition of the fresco; a composition which unwinds itself in a spiral round a segment of the Earth to lose itself in the profundity of Heaven. Carried away by mystic fervour on irresistible waves of music, the angelic orchestra plays on the balustrade which is the limit of the painted architecture, choirs of angels join the celestial musicians, and high in the radiant light which pervades each figure, appear the Divine Protagonists, amid such a swarm of cherubs, such an agitated flutter of draperies, such a great beating of wings, such a sunny tempest of clouds, that at first one has difficulty in discovering them. As in Vivaldi's finest sonatas, the singing rhythm illumines ever more vividly the climax of the vision, and the chromatic harmonies, among which yellow and violet predominate, become ever more limpid and crystalline, until they are lost in the vast light of infinite space (Fig. 43).

It was also in 1754 that Tiepolo, certainly with the help of Domenico, painted some chiaroscuro decorations in the Villa Volpato-Panigai at Nervesa (one of which, now in the Museum in Berlin, is, in fact, dated 1754), and probably in the same time bracket he frescoed, with Mengozzi-Colonna, the Villa Contarini at Mira, between Padua and Venice, where he depicted the *Reception of Henry III at the Villa Contarini*, which took place in 1574 – a fresco now removed to the Musée Jacquemart-André (Fig. 42). The frescoes in the Villa Soderini, later Berti, at Nervesa near Treviso, destroyed during the first world war in 1917, were also of about this date. These frescoes showed events connected with the Soderini family in Florence, but it was obvious that much was due to assistants and it was, in fact, possible to recognize the hand of Domenico and others. On the ceiling of the principal saloon was an *Apotheosis of the Soderini Family,* in which the painter's imagination once again soared into space, without hindrance or extraneous restraints (Fig. 44).

Since the name of his son Domenico has cropped up several times already, this is perhaps the best point at which to attempt to draw – in so far as it is here possible – a dividing line between father and son in their joint productions. There is no doubt that to his contemporaries 'Tiepolo' meant Giambattista, and if the son worked with his father, the result was considered as the production of the father, and the merit was his. In their own day, and, it may be added, until the beginning of the present century, the name 'Tiepolo' was a collective name, which embraced the work of Domenico as well as that of Lorenzo. Only recently has the figure of Domenico been isolated, while that of Lorenzo, the youngest son, still remains largely unknown, In the Villa Valmarana at Vicenza, Giambattista and Domenico worked at the same time in the *Palazzina* and the *Foresteria.* A fresco with a *Carnival Scene* in the *Foresteria* bears the name of Domenico Tiepolo and a date. This date had been wrongly read as 1737, and it was not possible to make this date agree with the known age of Domenico, who was then ten years old, whence it was inferred either that the painting was executed by the father, who had written his son's name on it to record their collaboration, or that Domenico, at ten years of age, was a prodigy unique in the history of art ! But as such precocity seemed to me inadmissible and since the style of the paintings in the Villa conflicted with the dating of 1737, meekly accepted *ab antiquo* by writers on Tiepolo, I went into the question and succeeded in establishing that the date should be read as 1757 – that is, twenty years later. Thus it was clear that Domenico Tiepolo, who signed this fresco, was in fact its real author, and on this stylistic basis I was able to reclaim for him other frescoes in the *Foresteria* and to re-arrange in this respect, much of the father's chronology.

In this Villa, which consists of two buildings, the father decorated five rooms, that is, all the principal ones in the *Palazzina* – the villa proper, occupied by the owners, the Counts Valmarana – while in the *Foresteria* (the part reserved for the guests) Domenico frescoed all the rooms except one, called the Sala dell'Olimpo, which was by Giambattista. In the paintings done by Domenico independently the themes alone (the Chinese Room, the Pastoral Room, the Gothic Room, the Room of the Masquerades with the *Charlatan* and the *Diorama;* Figs. 45-46) denote a different trend of taste, and an anticlassical spirit appears, a descriptive and anecdotic tendency – in short, a flavour midway between the Romantic and the Bourgeois which is poles apart from the idealistic style of Giambattista.

In the paintings of the *Palazzina* Giambattista appears in a new stylistic phase. Some of the themes which he had to treat were quite new ones, which compelled him to restudy figure compositions demanding immediate solutions. The preparatory drawings for many of these scenes have been preserved (Pls. 73 and 74), especially in the Victoria and Albert Museum, London, and in the Museo Civico in Trieste, and prove the lightning rapidity with which Giambattista crystallized the images of his fantasy. Tiepolo has now almost entirely abandoned the diagonal perspective schemes of composition dear to his youth; with few exceptions his figures now move on planes parallel to the wall. The return to Veronese's influence, already revived at Mira, is noticeable above all in the principal room, where, in the *Sacrifice of Iphigenia* both the architectonic and illusionistic structure, and the relationship between the figures are derived from Veronese. In the Room of the Iliad, and in that of the Aeneid, the artist develops a whole new body of heroic iconography; the single episode of *Venus abandoning Aeneas* suffices to show the ever fresh vein of his poetic invention. In the Rooms of the Orlando Furioso and of the Gerusalemme Liberata Giambattista played with the style of the French Rococo not only in the framing and in the rather frivolous and over-abundant ornament, but even in the way in which he managed the figures. But from that exotic contact (certainly made at Würzburg) he evolves hypersensitive colour combinations, sharp and heady, where fragile and delicate pastel tones, cornflower blues, thin yellows, now acid, now tending towards pearly grey, tender amaranthine lilacs, greens either glittering or liquid emerald, scintillate in incomparable variety. The Sala dell'Olimpo in the *Foresteria* is, in its simplicity, one of the most harmonious and balanced expressions of his art. The group of *Mars and Venus* and especially that of *Apollo and Diana,* conceived in an admirable equilibrium of masses – Apollo luminous in the light of the dawn, Diana half-hidden in the evening shadow – will

Fig. 47. MARS AND VENUS. Fresco, 1757. Vicenza, Villa Valmarana

Fig. 48. VENUS ABANDONS AENEAS. Fresco, 1757.
Vicenza, Villa Valmarana

Fig. 49. THE SACRIFICE OF IPHIGENIA. Fresco, 1757. Vicenza, Villa Valmarana

Fig. 50. APOLLO AND DIANA. Fresco, 1757. Vicenza, Villa Valmarana

Fig. 51. THE TRIUMPH OF TRUTH. Fresco, about 1757. Vicenza, Palazzo Trento-Valmarana, destroyed in 1945

Fig. 52. MERIT BETWEEN NOBILITY AND VIRTUE. Ceiling fresco, about 1758. Venice, Palazzo Rezzonico

Fig. 53. THE ASSUMPTION OF THE VIRGIN. Ceiling fresco. 1759.
Udine, Chiesa della Purità

Fig. 54. MARRIAGE ALLEGORY. Ceiling fresco. About 1758.
Venice, Palazzo Rezzonico

Fig. 55. ALLEGORY. Grisaille, about 1750–60. Zurich, Private Collection

always remain an outstanding example of the creative serenity of the artist. The superb air of these deities, their vivid and transparent tonality, that feeling for the quivering line, delicate and sensitive, all this represents a new conquest for Tiepolo in these years of ceaseless activity (Figs. 47-50).

The decoration of the grand saloon in the Palazzo Valmarana-Trento in Vicenza (unfortunately destroyed in the bombardments of 1945) can also be assigned to this period around 1757. On the ceiling Tiepolo frescoed four circular panels with allegories of the Arts, Music, Science and History, and a large central oval of the *Triumph of Truth over Falsehood,* in which Error, in the guise of a feeble old man with bandaged eyes, wanders blindly on a false path and Truth, nude, high among the clouds with the sun in her hand, condemns his aberrations and precipitates Falsehood head downwards towards Calumny, personified by a monstrous, repellent old hag with serpent legs – a pictorial image of powerful fantasy (Fig. 51) of which the artist has left us the first conception in two sheets of pen sketches in the Museum in Trieste.

On his return to Venice, Tiepolo began working for the Rezzonico family, who, during these years, had employed the architect Massari to alter their palace on the Grand Canal and were now enriching it with works of art. It is believed that Tiepolo finished the frescoes in the two rooms by 1758, a year of propitious events for the Rezzonico, since on the 18th January of that year the marriage took place of Lodovico Rezzonico with Faustina Savorgnan, while on the 13th July Cardinal Carlo was elected Pope. In one of these frescoes he took up the motive of the white quadriga, already developed at Würzburg, representing an allegory of the *Arrival of the Bride,* the *modelletto* for which is preserved in the Museo Civico in Verona; in the other is an *Allegory of Merit between Nobility and Virtue.* In the nuptial fresco the disposition of the two principal groups is new, since they are not on the same plane, as in Würzburg, but because of the restricted space, on two different perspective planes, outside and inside the cornice of the painted balustrade; and in the second fresco of *Merit* the iconographic motive of the Temple of Virtue is also new, and one which he will take up again in later commissions (Figs. 52, 54).

Tiepolo, who at thirty had created at Udine, in the Palazzo Dolfin, his first big cycle of frescoes in a private house, returned there after more than thirty years, this time with Domenico, to decorate the Cappella della Purità, and to his son he confided the chiaroscuro decoration of the walls. The account books of the church show that the admirable ceiling with the *Assumption* was painted by Giambattista between the 14th August and the 16th September, 1759, in the space of thirty-two days, reduced to twenty-eight at most if one takes into account Sundays and holidays: and he had more than a hundred square metres to cover. In this work he uses the compositional scheme of the Carmine ceiling, but with a different key of colour and a more nervous calligraphy. Tiepolo was now able to render, more than ever before, extreme delicacy of tone so that the figures become ever more evanescent, wrapped in an all-pervading iridescence of colour, completely new in the history of mural painting (Fig. 53).

This is exemplified in the *Triumph of Hercules* (Pl. 77), which the artist frescoed on the ceiling of the Palazzo Canossa in Verona in 1761, with the assistance of the Milanese Visconti for the ornamental parts, as is known from the *Componimenti poetici* dedicated to Tiepolo in that year by the Veronese writer Zaccaria Betti – an admirable fresco, which, in certain points of the composition, prefigures the frescoes in Madrid. So again in the ceiling of the Villa Pisani at Strà, with the *Apotheosis of the Pisani Family* (Pl. 78) which he frescoed between the autumn of 1761 and the first months of 1762; and this is one of his most successful imaginative compositions. The portraits of the members of the Pisani family are particularly noteworthy, some of them very keenly observed, and all, surely, done from life. On the left is Marina Pisani Sagredo, who presses close to her the young Almorò Pisani, and on the right his father Andrea, who had died a few years earlier; in the centre are the little cousins from the Venetian side of the family. The group of the lute players at the bottom, placed against the dark green of the pines is iconographically new and very beautiful – an exquisite passage in which the translucent flesh tones stand out against the bottle-green of the foliage and form a colour note of exciting strangeness.

But the *joie de vivre* which prompted these secular allegorical glorifications changed key – disappeared – when the artist was called upon to treat themes of religious emotion. Then he knew how to make other chords vibrate, more intimate and profound. Not that the eighteenth century in Venice could be said to be the time or the place most suited to promote religious contemplation, but Tiepolo's Catholic soul – through the resources of traditional mystical devotion – aroused itself anew each time that the artist called upon it. This happened, for example, when he was commissioned to paint for the church of the Grazie at Este the great altarpiece of *S. Thecla* (Pl. 75) which was placed upon the altar on Christmas Eve of 1759. In it he represented the Saint imploring an end to the plague and the Eternal who, receiving her prayers, descends from Heaven surrounded by angels and cherubs and puts the demon of evil to flight. A leaden atmosphere hangs over the city, and for all that there are a few intense flashes of colour in the robes of the Saint, all artistic sensuality is overcome by the aura of religion, and at the same time by the profound human sympathy. Passages of intense drama, such as that of the baby clinging to its dead mother, or the carrying away of the body of a plague victim in the background, are among the most touching examples of the art of Giambattista. In the *modelletto* for this picture, now in the Metropolitan Museum, New York, the emotional accents are interwoven in a continuous, delicate vibration of light and ashen colour (Col. Pl. VIII).

VI

MADRID

1762 – 1770

WHILE he was working on the frescoes of the Villa Pisani at Strà, Tiepolo was invited by Charles III of Spain to decorate the new Royal Palace, recently finished by the Turinese architect Giambattista Sacchetti, a pupil of Juvara. In a letter of the 12th December, 1761 he wrote – probably to Algarotti – that he could not do less than agree to the entreaties of the King, but that he would not be able to leave until the following February. He did not leave, however, accompanied by his painter sons, Domenico and Lorenzo, until the beginning of April, leaving to his son Giuseppe, a priest, the control of his household. His faithful assistant, Mengozzi-Colonna, now seventy-four years of age, remained in Venice and died there two years later. The journey made by land, via Barcelona, was slow and they arrived in Madrid only on the 2nd June, after nearly two months travelling. Giambattista, who was now sixty-six years old, was so fatigued by the journey that he had to take to his bed, in the house of the Venetian Ambassador. But he soon recovered and set to work.

First he set himself to fresco the Throne Room for which, in the first months of 1762, when still in Italy, he had painted the *modelletto,* which is probably identical with the canvas now in the National Gallery of Art in Washington (Pls. 79, 81). The general idea is the same as the staircase at Würzburg combined with some elements from the ceiling of the Villa Pisani. The ceiling is huge, measuring fully eleven by twenty-six metres, and Tiepolo frescoed it with the *Apotheosis of Spain* (Pls. 80, 82-90). There he gathered together all the creatures of his imagination: symbolical and mythological figures poised in the skies, winged genii and playful putti, Virtues in glory and Vices in impetuous flight, Faith wrapped in a white mantle and Fortitude with her tower, Apollo and Neptune, Ceres and Mercury, Bacchus and Ariadne, Vulcan and Saturn, Jove and Minerva, Eolus and Thetis, nereids, tritons, zephyrs, and in the centre, between the massive pyramid and the arc of the rainbow, right at the top, floating in the clear atmosphere which invests the whole, is Spain enthroned and surrounded by all the attributes that good government could desire. Placed above the cornice are fanciful groups representing Spanish provinces and the Quarters of the Earth, alternating in an attractively picturesque sequence of episodes, one of which represents Christopher

Columbus offering to Spain the spoils brought from America by the returning galleons. The vastness of the space to be frescoed, in conjunction with a height which does not permit one to take in the whole ceiling at a glance, compelled Tiepolo to compose in scattered elements and to thin out his groups over the immense sky, avoiding compact masses of figures. It is an excellent arrangement since it enables the spectator to enjoy, one at a time, the varied details of the vast decoration. In 1764 the fresco must have been finished, since that date, with the signature of the painter, can be read on the cornice.

Immediately after this, Tiepolo painted two other ceilings of lesser importance in the same Palace: in the Guardroom he frescoed a mythological allegory with *Aeneas conducted to the Temple of Immortality by Venus,* and in the Antecamara de la Reyna, or Saleta, a *Triumph of the Spanish Monarchy* (Figs. 58, 59).

For the *Aeneas* ceiling, Tiepolo painted two *modelletti,* both now in America and both of the same size. One is in Boston, the other in Cambridge, Mass., and they present considerable variations on the same theme: at the bottom is the forge of Vulcan, where the Cyclops are making the arms for Aeneas, and, higher up, the personification of Time as *Chronos,* which makes a bridge to the central group of Aeneas, accompanied by Victory and by Merit with the lion. On high appears Venus about to give him the plumed helmet prepared for him by Vulcan with which he will be able to enter the Temple of Immortality. Of the two sketches, the one in Cambridge is undoubtedly clearer in the composition and more harmonious as a whole, and this was, in fact, adapted for the fresco (Figs. 57, 60).

In these last two ceilings the sons collaborated but they adhered completely to their father's intentions, which remained unaltered and the painting indeed retains the spirited vivacity of the great Venetian's imagination. It may, however, be observed that compared with the ceiling of the Throne Room, these last two frescoes present less foreshortenings and in them there is a relatively small play of *di sotto in su* perspective. This has been imputed, though wrongly in my opinion, to the influence of Mengs. Nevertheless, it is easy to imagine that there was a certain rivalry between the two. Anton Raphael Mengs, standard bearer of Winckelmann's Neo-classic theory, preached the return to the antique, to simplicity, to calm composure. The ceilings which he painted in the same Royal Palace, without foreshortening and carried out in the taste of a resurrected (and frozen) Raphael, demonstrate the profound antithesis between his art and that of Giambattista. We know, moreover, who it was at Court who favoured Mengs at the expense of Tiepolo; it was Padre Joaquim de Electa, the King's confessor and the secret manager of Court affairs.

The story of Tiepolo's last years in Spain is a sad one. The great painter, at the end of one of the most brilliant careers that ever an artist had, found himself misunderstood and treated with hostility. When, after finishing the frescoes in the Royal Palace at the beginning of 1767, he declared that he would be willing to remain in the service of the King, and asked to be given commissions for paintings on canvas, such as he had executed for other Courts, he was able to obtain, it is true, through the good offices of the architect Antonio Sabbatini, who had just finished building the church of S. Pascal at Aranjuez, a commission for seven altarpieces for the church. But when they were ready Padre de Electa refused to receive either Giambattista or his sons – a sign of his manifest illwill. In fact, it was the same de Electa who shortly afterwards caused the paintings by Tiepolo to be removed from the altars and replaced by works by Mengs, Bayeu and Maella.

The seven canvases represented: *S. Pascal Baylon adoring the Holy Sacrament, The Immaculate Conception, S. Joseph, S. Peter of Alcantara writing, S. Francis of Assisi receiving the Stigmata, S. Charles Borromeo meditating on the Crucifix,* and *S. Antony of Padua with the Child Jesus.* Removed from the altars, they were distributed in the convent, and then dispersed, but today all may be traced, though in part mutilated. The *S. Pascal,* with the angel bringing the Sacrament is now, divided in two, in the Prado; the upper part with the angel has been there since 1872; the lower part entered the Museum only in 1926. In the Prado also are the *S. Francis of Assisi,* which, rolled up and damaged, was discovered in the depot in 1914; the *Immaculate Conception,* which has been recorded there since 1826; and finally a little fragment with an angel bearing a crown, which belonged to the *S. Joseph.* The *S. Joseph* proper, after having belonged to the Abbe Morèt, and been in the Heimann Coll., is now in the Museum in Detroit. The central part of the *S. Charles Borromeo* still exists, and was sold by the Parisian dealer Trotti to the Museum in Cincinnati. The *S. Peter of Alcantara* was recovered, rolled up but intact – it was always of an elliptical shape – from the depot of the Royal Palace in 1875, and is now in a room in the Palace. Finally, also in Madrid, the *S. Antony,* intact, passed from the Garcia family to the Señora Rodriguez-Bauza. And so the piety of posterity may mentally reunite in the solitary church at Aranjuez Tiepolo's seven pictures which the impious incomprehension of a friar had thought to destroy. The seven pictures are in most cases signed and autograph, and constitute one of the most profoundly religious series by Giambattista. There are no grand flights of imagination and the compositions are reduced to the essentials, but a heart-rending expression of faith shines from the faces of the Saints, some in ardent, ascetic ecstasy, others in austere meditation. For four of the seven canvases *modelletti* are known – for the *S. Pascal,* the *S. Francis,* the *S. Joseph,* and the *S. Charles Borromeo* (Pl. 91, Figs. 61-63), all in the collection of Count Seilern in London, and they are among the simplest and most sincere expressions of mystical contemplation ever realized by the art of Giambattista. A fifth modello, for the *Immaculate Conception,* has just been discovered in the collection of Lord Kinnaird in London.

During the years in Madrid Tiepolo also painted, for the Convent of Aranjuez, a large altarpiece of *S. James of Compostela on horseback,* now in the Museum in Budapest, a harmony of silvery and pearly tones, with broad swathes of blue in the drapery, the reflections and the sky (Fig. 64). He also produced, for an unknown destination, the *Abraham with the Angels,* now in the Prado, in which the artist takes up again, with great inward feeling, the theme frescoed so many years earlier in Udine.

Giambattista's activity must have been feverish in these last years, since in this period he executed many other works, some of which, for the Court of Russia, were sent from Spain; for example, the canvas for a ceiling representing *Mars and the Graces,* which was placed in the Oranienbaum Palace near Leningrad, where it still was before the war (and perhaps still is). Two other ceilings, one of a *Chariot of Venus and the Graces,* the other of a *Triumph of Hercules,* Tiepolo also painted during his Spanish residence, and they were engraved by his sons, but where they are now is not known. The *Triumph of Hercules* in the Thyssen Coll. in Lugano, painted by Domenico and then engraved by him, might perhaps have been the *modelletto* for one of these lost ceilings. In this period Domenico was completely identified with his father, in a form of absolute mimicry. Many other *modelletti* or sketches or just picturesque ideas were thrown off impetuously by the old magician with the tireless imagination; small canvases full of scintillating inspiration, extremely spirited, in which he released the pent up memories of the faraway joyous days of the Venetian age, as in the allegory of *Venus and Apollo* formerly in the Van Diemen Gallery in Berlin and now in the Becker-Rothschild Coll. in New York, or in the *Triumph of Venus* in the Prado. That world of mythology, literary, courtly, in which his fantasy had soared, without rest, without limit, and to which he had given form and colour, always new and various, that world continued to live in his brain ever fecund in new ideas. It continued to live as in a mythological fairy world, gushing up endlessly and almost of its own impulsion.

But the real soul of the painter, the soul of him who had created masterpieces of religious art, was withdrawing thoughtfully into itself. In a multitude of small canvases of sacred subjects, all referable to the Spanish period, this soul is reflected with a limpid sincerity of expression; the drawings and the sketches often allow us to see more deeply into the true spirit of the artist than do the large works, carefully calculated and finished. The religious feeling of the artist in some of these canvases becomes anxious, almost dramatic. Among so many, I should like to record a group of three works in the Pinto-Basto Coll. in Lisbon, which show a rapid crescendo. First, there are two scenes of the *Flight into Egypt,* in one of which he takes up again the motive of the angel with the boat, known from his drawings (a lovely one of which once belonged to Prince Orloff) and from the engravings by Domenico; in the other scene, however, the dominant element is the landscape – a tragic landscape, tormented and skeletal, such

Fig. 56. THE ENTOMBMENT. About 1762–70. Lisbon, Pinto Basto Collection

Fig. 57. APOTHEOSIS OF AENEAS. Sketch, about 1764–66. Boston, Museum of Fine Arts

Fig. 58. APOTHEOSIS OF AENEAS. Fresco, 1764–66. Madrid, Royal Palace, Guard Room

Fig. 59. APOTHEOSIS OF THE SPANISH MONARCHY. Fresco, 1764–66. Madrid, Royal Palace, Saleta

Fig. 61. SAINT CHARLES BORROMEO. Sketch, between 1767 and 1769.
London, Count Seilern Collection

Fig. 60. APOTHEOSIS OF AENEAS. Sketch, about 1764–66. Cambridge, Mass., Fogg Art Museum

Fig. 63. SAINT PASCAL BAYLON. Sketch, between 1767 and 1769.
London, Count Seilern Collection

Fig. 62. SAINT JOSEPH. Sketch, between 1767 and 1769.
London, Count Seilern Collection

Fig. 64. SAINT JAMES OF COMPOSTELA. Altar-piece, about 1767–70.
Budapest, Museum of Fine Arts

as one sees in certain parts of Spain and which presages Goya. In the third picture, of the *Entombment,* the religious feeling is once again completely inward, of a sad profundity, like a presage of death (Pls. 92, 93; Fig. 56).

On the 27th March, 1770, Giambattista Tiepolo died suddenly, at the age of seventy-four years. From the death certificate of the parish of S. Martín, in which he lived, it is clear that he was unable to receive the Sacraments. We know that he was a cheerful, frank man, with a noble soul; and his spirit is immortal. That the difficulties he encountered over the work for Aranjuez, and the hostility which his art increasingly met in Madrid, had embittered his last years and hastened his death, does not appear to be a rash judgement. After the discoveries at Pompeii and Herculaneum, Neo-classicism was knocking ever more insistently on the door with all its dogmatism and its frozen world of archaeological mirages, and it was Goya, with the sweep of his tragic humanity who finally exorcised it, after the short period dominated by Mengs. It was the same Goya whose links with Tiepolo no one any longer doubts. Giambattista had arrived in Spain at an age when it is difficult to be influenced; nevertheless, he underwent some, not from artists, but from nature, from the arid stony wastes of Old Castile which contribute no little to the intensification of the tones of azure, of tawny or silver grey, in the most significant works of these years. Perhaps, also, he was influenced by the austere Spanish Catholic atmosphere – since the artist is never completely insensitive to the environment in which he lives – as it appears in the severe canvases for Aranjuez, in which there is an unusual renunciation of spectacular effects.

But it must also be added that Tiepolo's influence in Spain was far from negligible. Even the painters from Mengs's circle felt it, and Bayeu and Maella, in the very altarpieces at Aranjuez which were substituted for the canvases of Giambattista, were inspired by their great predecessor. Don Vincente Lopez, having to fresco the Royal Chapel, leaned more to Tiepolo than to Mengs, as his sketches show even more clearly. Still more is this true of Goya. It was Tiepolo's ardent, impetuous spirit, irrepressible in its pictorial vitality, which was to capture the imagination of the great Aragonese; it was that sea of light diffused through the whole range of the rainbow, which stimulated the creative powers of Goya; it was his more than human and intoxicating sensuousness of colour, so close to reality, yet so metaphysical, with all the breathtakingly beautiful creatures of his imagination which kindled Goya's fantasy. He must certainly have seen the drawings and the etchings both of Giambattista and of Domenico; the *Education of the Infante Don Luis Antonio* (by Domenico), or some of the *Capricci,* explain better than anything else the origins of Goya's art in this respect.

The help given to Tiepolo by Domenico and Lorenzo during the Spanish period must indubitably have been considerable. But it is useless to try to conceal that it is extremely difficult to define it precisely. Above all, where the father made use of his sons in the frescoes in the Palace – and certainly he did – they worked from his cartoons with such fidelity that all their individuality of style was entirely suppressed; and the same may be said of the canvases for Aranjuez, where it is difficult to discover passages of unequal handling, and this notwithstanding that in some of his small independent canvases, Domenico appears extremely fertile in imagination, with his leaning towards a style at once romantic and narrative, pungent and astringent, which from his beginnings in the Villa Valmarana could be seen as clearly individual.

Domenico soon returned home. Lorenzo remained in Madrid, where after a few years he followed his father to the grave. Tiepolo had been buried in the crypt of the Saviour in his parish church of S. Martín. But the church was suppressed, the place no longer exists, the tomb of the Venetian has disappeared and with it even the memory of his ashes. But with the passage of time, the light of his art burns yet more brightly.

THE PLATES

1. VENUS WITH THE MIRROR. Canvas, about 1725. Milan, Conte Gerli Collection

2 THE SACRIFICE OF ABRAHAM. Ceiling fresco, about 1725–26. Udine, Archiepiscopal Palace

3. RACHEL HIDING THE IDOLS. Fresco, about 1725–26. Udine, Archiepiscopal Palace

4. ABRAHAM AND JACOB. Detail from Plate 3

5. RACHEL. Detail from Plate 3

6. THE ANGEL APPEARING TO SARAH. Fresco, about 1725–26. Udine, Archiepiscopal Palace

7. THE ANGELS APPEARING TO ABRAHAM. Fresco, about 1725–26. Udine, Archiepiscopal Palace

8. SARAH. Detail from Plate 6

9. ABRAHAM. Detail from Plate 7

10. THE JUDGEMENT OF SOLOMON. Fresco, about 1726–28. Udine, Archiepiscopal Palace

11. THE TEMPTATION OF SAINT ANTHONY. Canvas, about 1725. Milan, Brera

12. PHAETHON AND APOLLO. Fresco, 1731. Destroyed, formerly Milan, Palazzo Archinto

13. PHAETHON AND APOLLO. Canvas, 1731. Vienna, Academy of Fine Arts

14. HAGAR AND ISHMAEL. Canvas, 1732. Venice, Scuola di San Rocco

15. ISHMAEL. Detail from Plate 14

16. THE EDUCATION OF THE VIRGIN. Canvas, 1732.
Venice, Chiesa della Fava

17. THE VIRGIN IN GLORY ADORED BY APOSTLES AND SAINTS.
Canvas, 1734. Rovetta near Bergamo, Parish Church

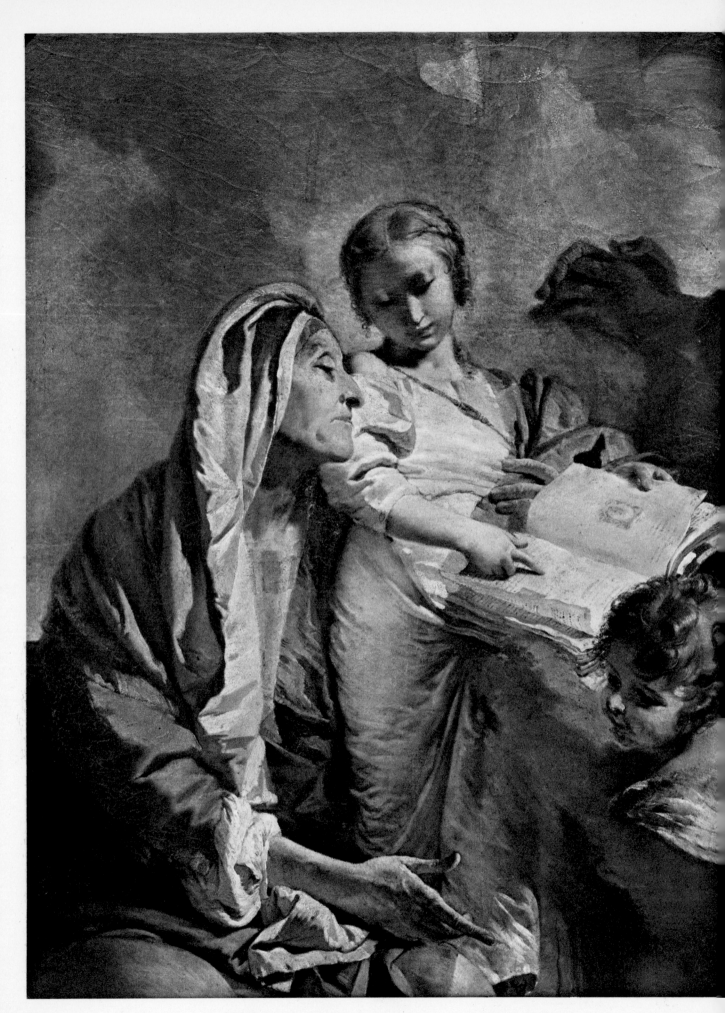

18. SAINT ANNE AND THE VIRGIN. Detail from Plate 16

19. SPECTATORS. Detail from Plate 17

20. SAINT PETER AND SAINT PAUL. Detail from Plate 17

III. SAINT DOMINIC INSTITUTING THE ROSARY. Fresco, 1737–39. Venice, Chiesa dei Gesuati

21. THE GATHERING OF THE MANNA. Canvas, about 1735–40. Verolanuova, Parish Church

22. THE GATHERING OF THE MANNA. Detail from Plate 21

23. THE GATHERING OF THE MANNA. Detail from Plate 21

24. ALLEGORY OF VICE AND VIRTUE. Pen drawing with water-colour. About 1740–45.
Florence, Horne Museum

25. MARINE GODDESS WITH A DOLPHIN. 1740. Detail from the fresco in the Palazzo Clerici, Milan

26. RIVER GODS AND NYMPHS. 1740. Detail from the fresco in the Palazzo Clerici, Milan

27. SATURN ABDUCTING VENUS. 1740. Detail from the fresco in the Palazzo Clerici, Milan

28. THE TRIUMPH OF AMPHITRITE. Canvas, about 1740. Dresden, Gallery

IV. DANAE. Canvas, just before 1736. Stockholm, University Museum

29. THE CONTINENCE OF SCIPIO. Canvas, 1743. Stockholm, National Museum

THE AGONY IN THE GARDEN

31. THE CROWNING WITH THORNS. Canvas, 1745–50. Hamburg, Kunsthalle

32. A SOLDIER. Detail from Plate 31

33. SOLDIERS. Detail from Plate 30

34. PORTRAIT OF ANTONIO RICCOBONO. Canvas, about 1745. Rovigo, Accademia dei Concordi

35. PORTRAIT OF GIOVANNI QUERINI. Canvas, about 1749 or later. Venice, Galleria Querini-Stampalia

36. ANTONIO RICCOBONO. Detail from Plate 34

37. GIOVANNI QUERINI. Detail from Plate 35

38. HEAD OF AN ORIENTAL. Canvas, 1750–60. Milan, Conte Rasini Collection

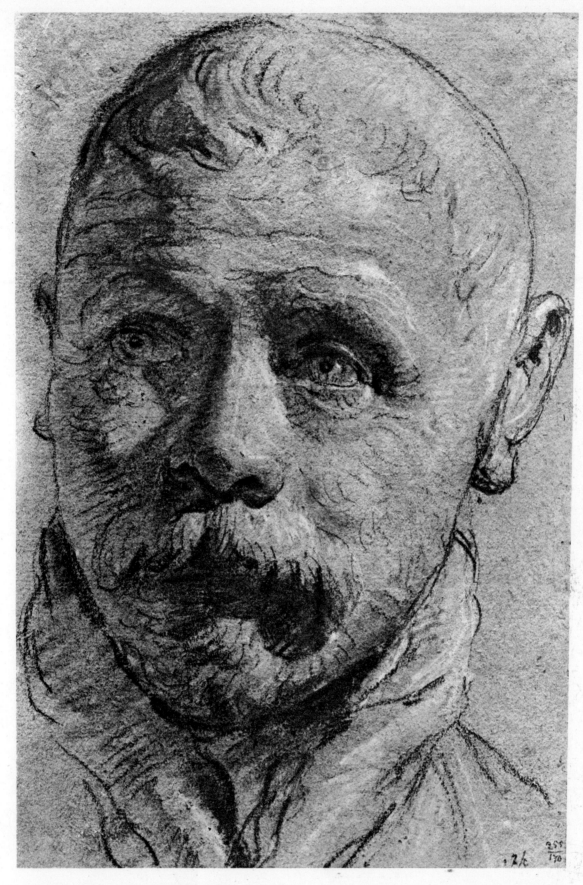

39. PORTRAIT OF PALMA GIOVANE, AFTER THE BUST BY ALESSANDRO VITTORIA.
Red chalk drawing on light-blue paper, about 1740–50. Milan, Conte Rasini Collection

40a. CARICATURE OF A CLERIC. Pen drawing
with sepia washes. About 1750–60. Paris, Ecole des Beaux-Arts

40b. CARICATURE OF A CAVALIERE.
Pen drawing with sepia washes. About 1750–60.
Milan, Museo Civico

40c. CARICATURE OF A SEATED OLD MAN.
Pen drawing with brown washes. About 1750–60. Venice, Bosisio Collection

40d. CARICATURE OF A GENTLEMAN.
Pen drawing with sepia washes. About 1750–60. Trieste, Museo Civico

41a. GROUP OF PULCINELLI.
Pen drawing with sepia washes. About 1740–50. Trieste, Museo Civico

41b. CARICATURE OF A CAVALIERE IN A DOMINO.
Pen drawing with sepia washes. About 1750–60. Milan, Museo Civico

41c. MASQUERADE.
Pen drawing with sepia washes. About 1740–50. Trieste, Museo Civico

41d. HUNCHBACKED PULCINELLI. Pen drawing
with sepia washes. About 1750–60. London, Mrs. Hilda Harris Collection

42. NEPTUNE OFFERING TO VENICE THE RICHES OF THE SEA. Canvas, about 1745–50. Venice, Palazzo Ducale

43. VENICE. Detail from Plate 42

44. NEPTUNE. Detail from Plate 42

45. HEAD OF AN OLD ORIENTAL. Pen drawing with sepia washes, about 1750–60.
Kansas City, William Rockhill Nelson Gallery

46. THE BANQUET OF ANTONY AND CLEOPATRA. Fresco, about 1745–50. Venice, Palazzo Labia

47. THE MEETING OF ANTONY AND CLEOPATRA. Fresco, about 1745–50. Venice, Palazzo Labia

48. THE MEETING OF ANTONY AND CLEOPATRA.
Detail from Plate 47

49. THE BANQUET OF ANTONY AND CLEOPATRA.
Detail from Plate 46

50. THE ADORATION OF THE MAGI. Canvas, 1753. Munich, Alte Pinakothek

51. THE MARTYRDOM OF SAINT AGATHA. Canvas, about 1745-50. Berlin, Kaiser Friedrich Museum

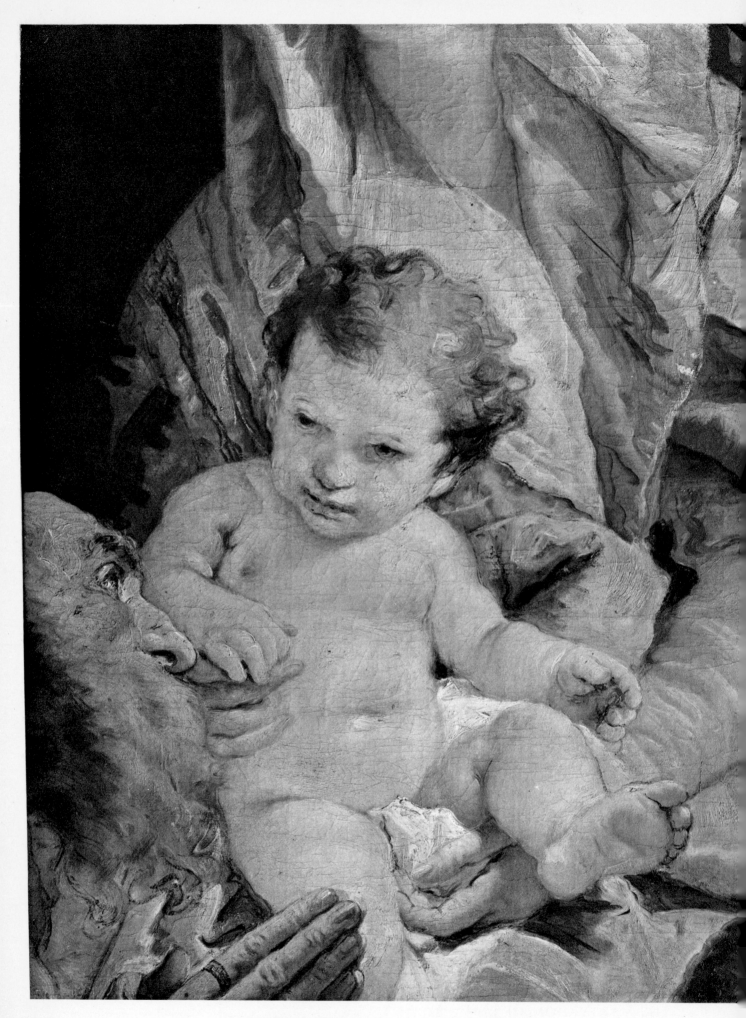

52. THE CHRIST CHILD. Detail from Plate 50

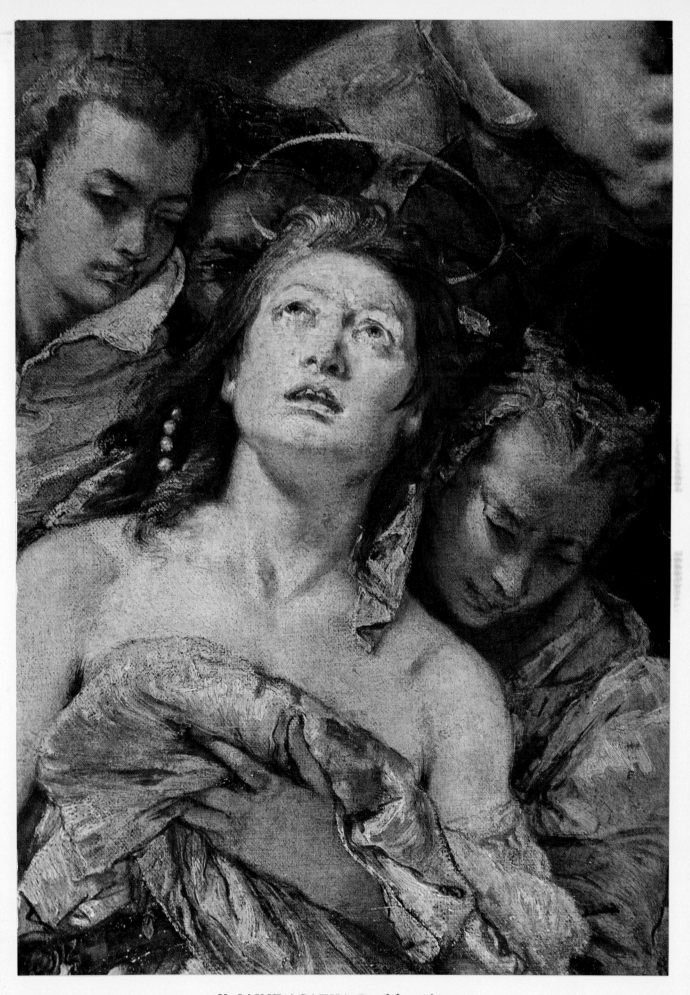

V. SAINT AGATHA. Detail from Plate 51

53. THE MAGI. Detail from Plate 50

54a. VIEW OF THE KAISERSAAL. 1751–52. Würzburg, Residenz

54b. VIEW OF THE KAISERSAAL. 1751–52. Würzburg, Residenz

55. VIEW OF THE STAIRCASE. 1752–53. Würzburg, Residenz

56. APOLLO CONDUCTING BEATRICE OF BURGUNDY

SSA. 1751–52. Fresco on the ceiling of the Kaisersaal. Würzburg, Residenz

57. 'AFRICA'. Detail from the fresco on the ceiling of the staircase. Würzburg, Residenz

58. 'AMERICA'. Detail from the fresco on the ceiling of the staircase. Würzburg, Residenz

59. WOMAN CARRYING A BASKET. Detail from Plate 58

VI. 'AMERICA'. Detail from Plate 58

60. 'AFRICA'. Detail from Plate 57

62. 'EUROPE'. Detail from the fresco on the ceiling of the staircase. Würzburg, Residenz

63. 'EUROPE'. Detail from the fresco on the ceiling of the staircase. Würzburg, Residenz

64. BARBAROSSA AWAITING HIS BRIDE. Detail from Plate 56

65. NYMPH AND RIVER GOD. Detail from Plate 64

66. APOLLO'S STEEDS. Detail from Plate 56

67. THE INVESTITURE OF BISHOP HAROLD. Fresco, 1752. Würzburg, Residenz, Kaisersaal

VII. THE MARRIAGE OF BARBAROSSA. Fresco, 1752. Würzburg, Residenz, Kaisersaal

68. TIEPOLO'S SELF-PORTRAIT WITH HIS SON DOMENICO AND ANOTHER ASSISTANT.
Detail from 'EUROPE'. Ceiling of the staircase. Würzburg, Residenz

69. RINALDO AND ARMIDA. Canvas, about 1750–55. Chicago, Art Institute

70. MOSES SAVED FROM THE WATERS. Canvas, about 1755-60. Edinburgh, National Gallery of Scotland

71. MOSES SAVED FROM THE WATERS. Detail from Plate 70

72. RINALDO AND ARMIDA. Detail from Plate 69

73. APOLLO. Pen drawing with sepia washes. 1757. London, Victoria and Albert Museum

74. DIANA. Pen drawing with sepia washes. 1757. Stuttgart, Kupferstichkabinett

75. SAINT THECLA DELIVERING THE CITY FROM THE PLAGUE.
Canvas, 1759. Este, Chiesa delle Grazie

VIII. SAINT THECLA DELIVERING THE CITY FROM THE PLAGUE.
Canvas, 1758. Sketch for the altarpiece at Este (Plate 75).
New York, Metropolitan Museum of Art

76. THE ANNUNCIATION. Pen drawing with sepia washes. 1760–70.   Paris, Private Collection

77. THE TRIUMPH OF HERCULES. Fresco, 1761. Verona, Palazzo Canossa

78. APOTHEOSIS OF THE PISANI FAMILY. Fresco, 1761–62. Strà, Villa Pisani

79. THE WORLD PAYS HOMAGE TO SPAIN.
Modello. Canvas, 1762. Washington, National Gallery of Art (Samuel H. Kress Collection)

80. TOWER OF FORTITUDE. Detail from the fresco of 1762–64 in the Throne Room of the Royal Palace, Madrid

81. DETAIL FROM PLATE 79

82. FAITH AND OTHER CHRISTIAN VIRTUES.
Detail from the fresco of 1762–64 in the Throne Room of the Royal Palace, Madrid

83. CHRISTOPHER COLUMBUS AND NEPT

om the fresco of 1762–64 in the Throne Room of the Royal Palace, Madrid

84 THE TRIUMPHS OF SPAIN. Detail from the fresco of 1762–64 in the Throne Room of the Royal Palace, Madrid

85. THE SPANISH PROVINCES. Detail from the fresco of 1762–64 in the Throne Room of the Royal Palace, Madrid

86. THE BOOTY OF COLUMBUS. Detail from the fresco of 1762–64 in the Throne Room of the Royal Palace, Madrid

87. MARINE DEITIES. Detail from the fresco of 1762–64 in the Throne Room of the Royal Palace, Madrid

88. JUBILANT ANGELS. Detail from the fresco of 1762–64 in the Throne Room of the Royal Palace, Madrid

89. SPAIN AND THE CHRISTIAN VIRTUES.
Detail from the fresco of 1762–64 in the Throne Room of the Royal Palace, Madrid

90. SPAIN ENTHRONED BETWEEN PEACE AND JUSTI

n the fresco of 1762–64 in the Throne Room of the Royal Palace, Madrid

91. SAINT FRANCIS. Canvas, about 1767. London, Count Antoine Seilern Collection

92. REST ON THE FLIGHT INTO EGYPT. Canvas, 1762–70. Lisbon, Alice Ferreira Pinto-Basto Collection

93. THE FLIGHT INTO EGYPT. Canvas, 1762–70. Lisbon, Edoardo Ferreira Pinto-Basto Collection

SELECTED BIBLIOGRAPHY

NOTES ON THE PLATES

LIST OF TEXT ILLUSTRATIONS

ACKNOWLEDGEMENTS

Grateful acknowledgement is made to the authorities of the following galleries for permission to reproduce paintings in their collections: The Museum of Fine Arts, Boston, Mass.; Isabella Stewart Gardner Museum, Boston, Mass.; The Art Institute of Chicago; The National Gallery of Scotland, Edinburgh; The National Gallery of Victoria, Melbourne; The Metropolitan Museum of Art, New York; The National Museum, Stockholm; The Kunsthistorisches Museum, Vienna; The National Gallery of Art, Washington, D.C.; The Hessische Treuhandverwaltung, Wiesbaden (pictures from the Kaiser Friedrich Museum, Berlin).

Credit is due to the following photographers: Croci, Bologna (Fig. 51); Alinari, Florence (Pls. 2, 3, 6, 7, 35, 48, 49, 78, Figs. 3, 4, 23, 24, 43, 53); Brogi, Florence (Pls. 26, 27); Prof. W. Hege, Gelsenkirchen (Pls. 55, 66, 67); Annan, Glasgow (Pls. 70, 71, Fig. 33); Kleinhempel, Hamburg (Pls. 30, 31); *The Times*, London (Fig. 35); Moreno, Madrid (Pls. 80, 83, 85–88, 90); Wunderlich, Madrid (Pls. 84, 89); Foto Marburg (Pls. 54a, 54b, 56, 57); Mari, Milan (Pl. 25); Farabola, Milan (Pl. 11); Zani, Milan (Fig. 18); Anderson, Rome (Pls. 21–23, 46, 47, Fig. 21); Sterle, Trieste (Pls. 4, 5, 8–10); Agenzia Fotografica Industriale, Venice (Pls. 16, 17, 19, 20, 37, 39, 41b, c, 42–44, 50–53, Figs. 6–8, 11, 13, 17, 20, 25, 31, 32, 37); Boehm, Venice (Pl. 75, Figs. 5, 44, 50); Cacco, Venice (Pls. 40a, b, c, 74, 76); Fiorentini, Venice (Pls. 1. 13, 14, 15, 18, 29, 32–34, 36, 38, 91, Figs. 1, 2, 19, 22, 29, 30, 52, 54, 60–63); Soprintendenza ai Monumenti, Venice (Figs. 10, 49); Soprintendenza ai Monumenti, Verona (Pl. 77); Gundermann, Würzburg (Pls. 61, 62, 68); Zwicker, Würzburg (Pls. 59, 60, 63–65).

Colour plates I, VI, VII were made from photographs taken by Prof. W. Hege, Gelsenkirchen. Colour plate IX is reproduced by courtesy of the National Gallery of Art, Washington. The photographs for the other colour plates were taken by Claudio Emmer, Milan.

SELECTED BIBLIOGRAPHY

1732   DA CANAL, V.: *Vita di Gregorio Lazzarini* (pub. by G. A. Moschini, Venice 1809)

1733   ZANETTI, A. M.: *Descrizione di tutte le pubbliche pitture di Venezia ecc.*, Venice 1733

1753   ORLANDI, P. A.: *Abecedario pittorico*, Venice 1753

1762   LONGHI, A.: *Compendio delle Vite dei Pittori Veneziani storici più rinomati ecc.*, Venice 1762

1792   ALGAROTTI, F.: *Lettere sulla Pittura*, vol. VIII, Venice 1792

1795–96, LANZI, L.: *Storia Pittorica d'Italia*, Bassano 1795–96

1806   MOSCHINI, G. A.: *Della Letteratura Veneziana*, vol. III, Venice, 1806

1851–56, SELVATICO, P.: *Storia estetico-critica delle arti del disegno*, Venice, 1851–56

1880   MOLMENTI, P.: *Les fresques de Tiepolo dans la Villa Valmarana*, Venice 1880 (the Italian edition is of 1928)

1885   MOLMENTI, P.: *Il Carpaccio e il Tiepolo*, Turin 1885

1894   BERENSON, B.: *Venetian Painters of the Renaissance*, New York–London 1894

1896   MOLMENTI, P.: *Acqueforti del Tiepolo*, Venice 1896

1897   MEISSNER, F. H.: *Tiepolo* (in Knackfuss Künstlermonographien), Leipzig 1897

1897   MOLFESE, G.–CENTELLI, A.: *Gli affreschi di G. B. Tiepolo*, Turin 1897

1898   DE CHENNEVIÈRES, H.: *Les Tiepolo* (Coll. des Artistes celèbres), Paris 1898

1902   MODERN, H.: *G. B. Tiepolo, eine Studie*, Vienna 1902

1906   BAUDI DE VESME, A.: *Le peintre graveur italien*, Milan 1806

1909   MOLMENTI, P.: *G. B. Tiepolo*, Milan 1909 (2nd ed., French, 1911)

1910   SACK, E.: *G. B. und D. Tiepolo*, Hamburg 1910

1919   VON KUTSCHERA-WOBORSKY, O.: *Tiepolo und Rom*, in 'Kunstchronik', 1919

1921   FIOCCO, G.: *G. B. Tiepolo* (Piccola Collezione d'Arte), Florence 1921

1922   VOSS, H.: *Ueber Tiepolos Jugendentwicklung*, in 'Kunst u. Künstler', 1922

1923   FOGOLARI, G.: *Dipinti giovanili di G. B. Tiepolo*, in 'Bollettino d'Arte, 1923

1924   OJETTI-DAMI-TARCHIANI: *La pittura italiana del 600 e del 700*, Milan 1924

1926   LORENZETTI, G.: *Venezia e il suo estuario*, Milan 1926

1927   VON HADELN, D.: *Handzeichnungen von Tiepolo*, Munich–Florence 1927, 2 vols.

1929   FIOCCO, G.: *La Pittura veneziana del Seicento e Settecento*, Bologna 1929

1929   SANCHEZ-CANTON, J.: *Bocetos y dibujos de Tiepolo*, in 'Archivio Español de Arte y Arqueologia', 1929

1931   FOGOLARI, G.: *Il bozzetto del Tiepolo per il trasporto della Santa Casa di Loreto*, in 'Bollettino d'Arte', 1931

1931   DE VITO-BATTAGLIA, S.: *Il bozzetto del Tiepolo per il soffitto della Sala delle Guardie a Madrid*, Rome 1931

1931   VENTURI, L.: *Pitture italiane in America*, Milan 1931 (the English edition is of 1933)

1934   MORASSI, A.: *The Young Tiepolo*, in 'The Burlington Magazine', 1934

1935   MORASSI, A.: *More about the Young Tiepolo*, in 'The Burlington Magazine', 1935

1936   ARSLAN, W.: *Studi sulla Pittura del primo Settecento Veneziano*, in 'La Critica d'Arte', 1936

1936   COLETTI, L.: *Zwei Entwürfe von Tiepolo*, in 'Pantheon', 1936

1937   MORASSI, A.: *An Unknown Early Work by G. B. Tiepolo*, in 'The Burlington Magazine', 1937

1938   MORASSI, A.: *Yet More about the Young Tiepolo*, in 'The Burlington Magazine', 1938

1939   GOERING, M.: *G. B. Tiepolo*, in 'Thieme u. Becker Künstlerlexikon', Leipzig 1939, vol. XXXIII

1940   HEGEMANN, H. W.: *G. B. Tiepolo*, Berlin 1940

1940   FIOCCO, G.: *Pitture del Settecento Italiano in Portogallo*, Rome 1940

1941   MORASSI, A.: *G. B. e D. Tiepolo alla Villa Valmarana*, in 'Le Arti', 1941

1941   SCIERBATCHEVA, M.: *The Hermitage Tiepolos from Palazzo Dolfin*, article, in Russian, Leningrad 1941

1941   MORASSI, A.: *Domenico Tiepolo*, in 'Emporium', 1941

1941   PALLUCCHINI, R.: *Gli incisori veneti del Settecento* (Exhibition Catalogue), Venice 1941

1942   MORASSI, A.: *Novità e precisazioni sul Tiepolo*, in 'Le Arti' (two articles), 1942

1942   LORENZETTI, G.: *La pittura veneziana del Settecento*, Novara 1942

1942   VIGNI, G.: *Disegni del Tiepolo*, Padua, 1942

1943   MORASSI, A.: *Tiepolo*, Bergamo, 1943 (2nd edition, 1950)

1943   HETZER, TH.: *Die Fresken Tiepolos in der Würzburger Residenz*, Frankfurt a. M., 1943

1943   FERNANDEZ, J.: *Tiepolo, Mengs, and Don Raphael Ximeno y Planes*, in 'Gazette des Beaux-Arts', 1943

1945   MORASSI, A.: *Tiepolo e la Villa Valmarana*, Milan 1945

1945   PALLUCCHINI, R.: *Gli affreschi di G. B. e G. D. Tiepolo alla Villa Valmarana*, Bergamo 1945

1946   LORENZETTI, G.: *Il quaderno del Tiepolo al Museo Corrèr di Venezia*, Venice 1946

1947   GRABAR, I.: *The Tiepolos in Archangel and Tiepolo's Self-portrait*, article in Russian; in 'Art', II, Moscow 1947

1951   VIGNI, G.: *Tiepolo*, Florence 1951

1951   PIGNATTI, T.: *Tiepolo*, Milan 1951

1951   MAZZARIOL-PIGNATTI, *Itinerario tiepolesco*, Venice 1951

1951   WATSON, F. J. B.: *Eighteenth Century Venice* (Exhibition Catalogue), London 1951

1951   BERENSON, B.: *G. B. Tiepolo*, in 'L'Illustrazione italiana', 1951

1951   DELOGU, G.: *Tiepolo*, Bergamo 1951

1951   BARBANTINI, N.: *Tiepolo*, in 'Arti e Costume', Milan 1951

1952   RICHARDSON, E. P.: *Venice 1700–1800* (Exhibition Catalogue), Detroit, Mich. U.S.A. 1952

1952   CAILLEUX, J.: *Tiepolo et Guardi* (Exhibition Catalogue), Paris 1952

1953   SANCHEZ-CANTON, J.: *J. B. Tiepolo en España*, Madrid 1953

1953   PITTALUGA, M.: *Acquafortisti Veneziani del Settecento*, Florence 1953

NOTES ON THE PLATES

I
VENUS WITH THE MIRROR

Milan, Count Gerli Collection. Canvas, 38 × 48 cm.; about 1725.

A charming early work which shows the beginning of a personal style emerging from the influence of Piazzetta, Ricci and Bencovich. The composition is less heavy than the earliest works and a clearer light invests the scene. The style is very close to the *Temptation of Saint Antony* in the Brera Gallery (Plate 11) and, as the two pictures are almost identical in size, it may be that they both belong to a cycle of small paintings executed by Tiepolo in his Udine period. This painting was formerly ascribed to the School of Tiepolo but was identified as an original in 1949.

Exhibited in Venice 1951.

2-10
FRESCOES IN THE ARCHIEPISCOPAL PALACE

Udine, 1725-1728

These frescoes are recorded in the early literature and form the first great fresco cycle painted by Giambattista. It was commissioned by Dionigi Dolfin, who died in 1734. Gerolamo Mengozzi-Colonna collaborated with Tiepolo in the painting of the ornamental and perspective parts. The decoration of the palace began with the Grand Staircase and there is a reference to this in a letter of the 30th July, 1725. In the centre there is a fresco of the *Fall of the Rebel Angels* and around it are some monochromes representing eight stories from Genesis. The frescoes of the gallery were painted at about the same time as the staircase, about 1725-6. On the main wall is the *Angel appearing to Sarah*, *Rachel hiding the Idols* and the *Angels appearing to Abraham*. The three medallions on the ceiling represent the *Sacrifice of Abraham*, *Hagar in the desert* and *Jacob's Dream*. On the main wall of the gallery there are also two painted medallions in violet and ochre grisaille on a gold ground with the *Meeting of Esau and Jacob* and *Jacob wrestling with the Angel*. Between the windows on the wall facing the frescoes there are imitation statues of six prophetesses in greenish monochrome.

It has been suggested by some critics that some of the scenes in the gallery were painted by pupils or assistants,

but it seems very evident that everything is by Tiepolo himself. Soon afterwards (about 1727 or 1728) Tiepolo also frescoed the Sala Rossa in the same palace with the *Judgment of Solomon* which is signed in the lower right corner. The Sala has four medallions of prophets. The date 1733 which Modern and Molmenti thought they could read on a book held by one of the prophets does not exist. The cycle has been dated at about 1720–25 but the contemporary letter mentioned above and the style of the frescoes make a date about 1725–28 more probable.

11
THE TEMPTATION OF SAINT ANTONY

Brera, Milan. Canvas, 40 × 47 cm.; about 1725.

Exhibited in Venice in 1929 with an attribution to Tiepolo after having passed as a work by Francesco Fontebasso. The style of the picture clearly recalls that of the *Venus with the Mirror* (Plate 1).

Exhibited in Venice 1929, 1951.

12
PHAETHON AND APOLLO

Fresco, formerly in the Palazzo Archinto, Milan, but destroyed during the last war. About 7 × 9 metres. 1731.

This is one of four scenes painted by Tiepolo in the Palazzo Archinto. One of the frescoes – that in the principal saloon – was dated 1731 and the cycle is also mentioned in Da Canal's book of 1732.

In the principal saloon of the palace Tiepolo represented *The Triumph of the Arts* and in the other saloons there were frescoes of *Phaethon and Apollo*, *Perseus and Andromeda* and *Juno with Fortuna and Venus*. This is the first great fresco cycle which Tiepolo executed outside Venetian territory. It has been suggested that the smaller scenes are earlier in date than the *Triumph of the Arts* of 1731, but there is no doubt that all of them are contemporary.

13
PHAETHON AND APOLLO

Vienna, Academy of Fine Arts. Canvas, 67.8 × 52.5 cm.; 1731.

Modelletto for the ceiling of the Palazzo Archinto, Milan. There is another sketch of the same subject in the Bowes

Museum at Barnard Castle and both have to be considered first ideas for the fresco. The colour is strong with glaring yellows, roses and oranges. The impasto has a rather sandy quality and the outlines are broken and discontinuous. The facial types with rather deep-set eyes and large mouth are characteristic of Tiepolo's style at this period.

Exhibited in Venice 1951.

14-15
HAGAR AND ISHMAEL

Venice, Scuola di San Rocco. Canvas, 140 × 132 cm.; 1732.

This picture and its pendant, *Abraham and the Angels*, were lost for many years. After they were rediscovered both were put in the Upper Hall of the Scuola di San Rocco. The date 1732 is based upon formal and stylistic analogies with the *Adoration of the Christ Child* in the Sacristy of the Canons in St. Mark's, Venice, which is mentioned by Zanetti in 1733, specifying that the picture was put in St. Mark's in 1732. *Hagar and Ishmael* clearly shows the influence of Piazzetta, which serves to confirm that Tiepolo's style was much more advanced in fresco than in his oil paintings.

Exhibited in Venice 1945, Lausanne 1947, Venice 1951.

16, 18
THE EDUCATION OF THE VIRGIN

Venice, Chiesa della Fava. Canvas, 362 × 200 cm.; 1732.

This altarpiece is not mentioned by Da Canal, writing in 1732, but it is recorded in the Chiesa della Fava by Zanetti, writing in 1733.

Exhibited in Venice 1896 and 1951.

17, 19, 20
THE VIRGIN IN GLORY
ADORED BY APOSTLES AND SAINTS

Rovetta, near Bergamo, Parish Church. Canvas 378 × 134 cm.; 1734.

The altarpiece was painted in 1734 and placed in the church in 1736, in a rich frame of columns and statues by Andrea Fantoni of Rovetta. The style of this large painting is clearly linked with that of the fresco cycle in the Villa Loschi al Biron which is mentioned in one of Tiepolo's letters of 1734. A modello (or rather a first idea) for the altarpiece is in the Poldi-Pezzoli Museum, Milan.

Exhibited in Venice 1951.

21-23
THE GATHERING OF THE MANNA

Verolanuova, Parish Church. Canvas, 10 × 5.25 metres About 1735-40.

The Parish Church at Verolanuova contains the two larges canvases ever painted by Tiepolo – the *Gathering of th Manna* and the *Sacrifice of Melchisedec*. The unusually larg size of these two pictures may perhaps be due to the fac that there are two other very large pictures by Andre Celesti in the same church.

There is an old tradition that the contract for these picture was preserved in the archives of Count Gambara i Verolanuova and that the price paid was ten thousand lire It seems quite likely that Count Gian Franceso Gambara who was appointed *podestà* of Verolanuova in 1735, shoul have met Tiepolo in Venice, where there was a palac belonging to the Gambara family. The Count often visite Venice and it is probable that he commissioned the altar pieces for his parish church on one such visit.

The date of these canvases is somewhat controversial an varies from 1740 to 1759, although a date of 1725-30 ha also been advanced on purely stylistic grounds. The style however, seems to confirm rather than to disprove th tradition of a commission from Count Gambara abou 1735-40.

24
ALLEGORY OF VICE AND VIRTUE

Florence, Horne Museum. Pen drawing with water colour about 1740-45.

Tiepolo was an enormously productive draughtsman an his drawings help us to understand the way in which h evolved a pictorial idea. He made a number of differen drawings for the same composition, each of them showing a further stage in the development of the idea and each o them of an irresistible imaginative power. This drawing belongs to the period immediately after 1740 when his pe drawings seem to catch and summarize essential forms an movements. The style of the drawing is close to that of th fresco in the Palazzo Clerici in Milan of 1740.

25-27
MARINE GODDESS WITH A DOLPHIN,
RIVER GODS AND NYMPHS,
SATURN ABDUCTING VENUS

Details from the ceiling fresco in the Palazzo Clerici, Milan, 1740.

This palace passed in 1736 to the famous Marshal of the Empress Maria Theresa, Giorgio Antonio Clerici, who immediately set about transforming it. The redecoration had not been finished by 1738 as Lattuada (whose last volume on Milan came out in that year) does not mention it. Clerici sent for Tiepolo as soon as the palace was ready, and an anonymous poem says that Tiepolo was painting here in 1740.

On the vault of the gallery there is a fresco of the *Course of the Sun on Olympus* (22 × 5.40 metres). An impressive self-portrait of Tiepolo appears on the cornice of the fresco, below a flying putto holding a palette.

The ceiling suffered from damp during the war and is not now in very good condition.

28
THE TRIUMPH OF AMPHITRITE

Formerly Dresden, Gallery. Canvas, 188 × 442 cm.; about 1740.

Taken by the Russians in 1945 and now in Moscow. This was one of a cycle of four pictures of the Four Elements. Three of the four are known, the other two being *Juno and Luna* and *Bacchus and Ariadne* now in the Timken Collection in New York. These canvases were in the Villa Girola near Como until about 1880, when they were sold to the Viennese dealer Artaria, in whose store they lay until 1900 when their importance was recognized.

The almost neo-classical flavour of the compositions has led many critics into wrongly believing them to be by the hand of some other painter.

There is a sketch related to the *Triumph* in the Collection of Edoardo Ferreira Pinto-Basto in Lisbon which is a workshop copy; another copy is in the Museum in Trieste.

29
THE CONTINENCE OF SCIPIO

Stockholm, National Museum. Canvas, 60 × 43 cm.; 1743.

Sketch for the fresco in the Villa Cordellina at Montecchio Maggiore and pendant to the sketch of the *Family of Darius before Alexander*, which is now in the collection of Mario Crespi in Milan.

The frescoes, which still survive, are referred to in a letter dated 26th October, 1743, to Count Algarotti, in which Tiepolo writes that he had almost finished the paintings in the villa.

Exhibited in Venice 1951.

30-33
THE AGONY IN THE GARDEN, THE CROWNING WITH THORNS

Hamburg, Kunsthalle. Two canvases, each 79 × 90 cm.; about 1745-50.

According to the engraving by Pietro Monaco the *Agony in the Garden* – or another very close replica – was executed for the Venetian Giacomo Concolo, while the pendant is said to have been painted for Count Algarotti. In fact, the two canvases must have been very well known in Tiepolo's own day as there are a great many versions and copies of them. These include versions of the *Agony* in Munich, Ihrl Collection, and in the University Museum at Würzburg (which is by Domenico) as well as another workshop copy in the Museum at Athens. There are copies of the *Crowning* in the Museum at Vicenza and in the Kleinberger Collection in Paris as well as other copies of the two pictures in Paris, Venice and elsewhere.

The Hamburg pictures belong to a series of Passion pictures of which other examples are *The Last Supper* in the Louvre (Fig. 24), the *Crucifixion* in St. Louis (Fig. 25) and the *Crucifixion* in Vierhouten, Holland.

The usual date given to the canvases is about 1737-40 but they seem to be of a somewhat later period.

Exhibited in Venice 1951.

34, 36
PORTRAIT OF ANTONIO RICCOBONO

Rovigo, Accademia dei Concordi. Canvas, 120 × 90 cm.; about 1745.

The portrait was probably commissioned about 1745, when the Academy is known to have ordered portraits of famous men from other painters. Antonio Riccobono was a man of letters (Rovigo 1541-Padua 1599) who was appointed Professor at the University of Padua in 1571. The eighteenth-century guide books contain a good deal of information about this picture, which is one of the very few examples of Tiepolo as a portrait painter.

Exhibited in Florence 1911, Paris 1919, Venice 1946 and 1951.

35, 37
PORTRAIT OF GIOVANNI QUERINI

Venice, Galleria Querini-Stampalia. Canvas, 235 × 158 cm.; about 1749 or later.

When this vivid and sharp interpretation of character was

exhibited in Venice in 1896, it was first proposed to identify the sitter as a member of the Querini family, an identification which has passed unchallenged until very recently. This masterpiece is generally dated some years later than the *Antonio Riccobono*, that is at about 1749 or even later (1750–60).

Exhibited in Venice, 1896, Florence 1922, Venice 1929, London 1930, Paris 1935, Belgrade 1938, Lausanne 1947, and Venice 1951.

38
HEAD OF AN ORIENTAL

Milan, Conte Rasini Collection. Canvas, 43×35 cm.; about 1750–60.

It is probable that Tiepolo painted the numerous *Oriental Heads* in the years after 1750, perhaps with the same intention of forming a repertory of characteristic types that had induced Piazzetta to produce his *Heads*, later engraved by Pitteri. Tiepolo's *Heads* were etched by Domenico and printed in two series of thirty engravings each, after the death of Giambattista. The two volumes were dedicated to Alvise Tiepolo, Venetian Ambassador to the Pope, and were entitled *Raccolta di teste . . . dipinte dal Sig. Gio. Batta Tiepolo Pittore veneto al serviggio di S.M. Carlo morto in Madrid l'anno 1770, incise da Gio. Domenico suo Figlio*. Many critics have supposed that Domenico engraved the *Heads* from pictures by himself and not from his father's but it is more likely that the great majority of them were painted by Giambattista. As a rule they represent old orientals with beards and turbans or wearing furs with golden chains and jewels, some of which evidently show the influence of Rembrandt. There is a group of interesting drawings of such men in the Museum at Trieste.

Exhibited in Rome 1941, and Venice 1951.

39
PORTRAIT OF PALMA GIOVANE, AFTER THE BUST BY ALESSANDRO VITTORIA

Milan, Conte Rasini Collection. Red chalk drawing on light-blue paper, 25.5×17 cm.; about 1740–50.

The drawing represents the terracotta of Palma Giovane by Alessandro Vittoria of which one example – possibly the original, which once belonged to Tiepolo himself – was in the van Dirksen collection in Berlin. Tiepolo made a number of drawings of this head, another one being in the Harris collection, London, and it is an interesting fact that

Tiepolo, for all his skill as a draughtsman, continued to draw from sculpture as Tintoretto had done before him. Such drawings confirm Da Canal's statement that he wa commissioned to make drawings as well as paintings.

40a
CARICATURE OF A CLERIC

Paris, École des Beaux-Arts. Pen drawing with sepia washes; about 1750–60.

One of a large group of caricatures by Giambattista, who invented this as a sort of counterpart to his more serious work. The genre was later developed still further by Domenico, who in the Villa Valmarana shows his ability to catch the humorous side of mankind (Figs. 45–46), and who in his later years became an impressive satirist.

40b
CARICATURE OF A CAVALIERE

Milan, Museo Civico. Pen drawing with sepia washes about 1750–60.

It seems likely that drawings of this type inspired Domenico in his frescoes at the Villa Valmarana and in paintings such as the *Minuet* or the *Quack Doctor* in the Louvre.

40c
CARICATURE OF A SEATED OLD MAN

Venice, Bosisio Collection. Pen drawing with brown washes. 23×16.5 cm.; about 1750–60.

Exhibited in Venice 1951.

40d
CARICATURE OF A GENTLEMAN

Trieste, Museo Civico. Pen drawing with sepia washes. 22.9×17.7 cm.; about 1750–60.

The group of caricatures in the Museo Civico at Trieste was bequeathed by Count Segrè-Sartorio, and is one of the richest in existence.

41a
GROUP OF PULCINELLI

Trieste, Museo Civico. Pen drawing with sepia washes. 28×20.8 cm.; about 1740–50.

The style of this drawing is related to those which can be dated in the fourth decade of the century. This type of drawing was also adopted by his son Domenico in a number of humorous designs, the most famous of which was the album with 104 *Divertimenti per li ragazzi* now dispersed in various museums and private collections.

41b
CARICATURE OF A CAVALIERE IN A DOMINO

Milan, Museo Civico. Pen drawing with sepia washes; about 1750–60.

See note on Plate 40b.

41c
MASQUERADE

Trieste, Museo Civico. Pen drawing with sepia washes; 32.7 × 26 cm.; about 1740–50.

One of the most charming *Masquerade* drawings by Giambattista. The stylistic quality is ample proof that it is autograph.

41d
HUNCHBACKED PULCINELLI

London, Mrs. Hilda Harris Collection. Pen drawing with sepia washes; about 1750–60.

Stylistically of a later period than Plate 41a and closely related to some Pulcinelli pictures which Tiepolo painted in the 1750's, such as those in the Cailleux Collection in Paris or the Besnard Collection, also in Paris.

42–44
NEPTUNE OFFERING TO VENICE THE RICHES OF THE SEA

Venice, Palazzo Ducale. Canvas, 111 × 259 cm.; about 1745–50.

Overdoor in the *Sala delle quattro Porte*. The picture was sent to Naples for an exhibition in 1940 and was carried off to Germany. It was recovered and returned to the Doge's palace in 1948.

Exhibited in Paris 1919, Venice 1929, Naples 1940, Venice 1951.

45
HEAD OF AN OLD ORIENTAL

Kansas City, William Rockhill Nelson Gallery. Pen drawing with sepia washes; 24,7 × 19,7 cm.; about 1750–60.

One of the series of drawings of *Oriental Heads*, sketched

by Giambattista for his numerous pictures of the same subject. There are many similar drawings in the Museum of Trieste and in other collections.

46–49
THE BANQUET OF ANTONY AND CLEOPATRA and THE MEETING OF ANTONY AND CLEOPATRA

Venice, Palazzo Labia. Frescoes, about 1745–50.

This is the most famous cycle of frescoes painted by Tiepolo for a private palace. The splendid building was erected between 1720 and 1750, the façade towards S. Geremia being by the architect Tremignan and the one towards Canareggio by Andrea Cominelli.

The Banquet contains a remarkable self-portrait by Tiepolo; he is represented standing in profile near the Moor, looking at the spectator. The figure at his left is traditionally supposed to be his collaborator Mengozzi-Colonna.

The cycle used to be dated 1757 on the basis of a false date inscribed on the *Banquet*. A date of about 1745 was suggested on the grounds of some details in the construction of the palace itself. The style of the frescoes is close to the cycle in the Villa Cordellina of 1743 and it may be assumed that Tiepolo began to work in the palace between 1745 and 1750.

Some small damages suffered during the recent war have now been repaired.

There is a preparatory sketch for the *Meeting* in the National Gallery of Scotland, Edinburgh (Fig. 33), and one for the *Banquet* in the Museum at Stockholm (Fig. 32).

50, 52, 53
THE ADORATION OF THE MAGI

Munich, Alte Pinakothek. Canvas, 405 × 211 cm.; 1753.

Executed during Tiepolo's stay in Würzburg. Signed and dated; GIO. B. TIEPOLO. F.A. 1753.

This large altarpiece was painted for the church of the Benedictine Convent at Schwarzach. Tiepolo was paid 432 florins for it. Meusel in his diary (*Miscellaneen artistischen Inhaltes*, Erfurt, 1779) describes the picture, and notes that it was treated in the style of Veronese.

There are said to be two first ideas for the altarpiece, one in the Metropolitan Museum, New York, and the other in the Wallraf Richartz Museum in Cologne, but the first does not seem to be certainly a sketch for this altarpiece and the other is clearly a derivation from it, by Domenico.

Exhibited in Venice 1951.

51
THE MARTYRDOM OF SAINT AGATHA

Berlin, Kaiser Friedrich Museum. Canvas, 184 × 131 cm.; about 1745–50.

Said to have been painted for the High Altar of the church of St. Agatha belonging to the Benedictine Nuns at Lendinara. The picture was later in the Munro Collection, London, from which it was bought for Berlin in 1878. Tiepolo painted another version of the same subject for an altarpiece still in the Basilica del Santo at Padua, commissioned on the 27th December, 1734, and put in place in 1737. The Berlin picture is stylistically more advanced as well as more dramatic in feeling and must have been painted immediately before the Würzburg period.

A painting in the Correr Museum at Venice is believed to be the preparatory sketch, but it is not by Tiepolo himself.

Exhibited in Venice 1951.

54-68
FRESCOES

Würzburg, Residenz.

The sumptuous residence of the Prince-Bishop was begun under Johann Philip Franz von Schoenborn (appointed from 1719 to 1749), and was completed only in 1752. It is a work of the great architect Balthasar Neumann (1687–1753). Tiepolo accepted the invitation of the Prince-Bishop Carl Philip von Greiffenklau on the 12th October, 1750, and arrived with his sons Domenico and Lorenzo on the 12th December.

The first part of the decoration to be carried out was the ceiling of the Kaisersaal, with *Apollo conducting Beatrice of Burgundy to Barbarossa*, finished on the 8th July, 1751. The two scenes on the walls, representing the *Marriage of Barbarossa* and the *Investiture of Bishop Harold*, were finished in July, 1752. In this second scene Tiepolo painted a portrait of the Prince-Bishop as Bishop Harold, and signed and dated the fresco GIO. BATTA TIEPOLO, 1752.

After finishing the Kaisersaal Tiepolo signed a contract on the 29th July, 1752, for the staircase, for which he was paid twelve thousand florins. The ceiling represents *Olympus with the four quarters of the earth and allegories*. This is signed and dated G.BTTA TIEPOLO 1753 below the pyramid which symbolizes Egypt. This fresco contains another portrait of Carl Philip, supported by flying putti and genii above the symbol of Europe. In the same palace Domenico painted four overdoors for which he was paid one hundred ducats.

On the 8th November, 1753 Tiepolo and his sons returned to Venice.

69, 72
RINALDO AND ARMIDA

Chicago, Art Institute. Canvas, 175 × 210 cm.; about 1750–55.

One of the four scenes from the story of Rinaldo and Armida in the Art Institute at Chicago, which were originally in the palace of the Counts Serbelloni at Milan. The same subject was also painted by Tiepolo in Würzburg and at the Villa Valmarana.

These four paintings were dated incorrectly, because of the false reading of the date on the Valmarana fresco (read as 1737 instead of 1757). The Art Institute pictures were probably painted after those once in Würzburg and now in Munich (1751–53), and before those in the Villa Valmarana. These scenes are more free and brilliant than those executed in 1751–53 but they have not yet the refined and slightly frivolous quality, close to French Rococo, which characterizes the style of the Villa Valmarana.

There is an engraving by Domenico of the *Rinaldo Enchanted by Armida* and an etching by Lorenzo of the *Rinaldo and Armida Surprised*.

Exhibited in Chicago 1933, 1934, 1938.

70, 71
MOSES SAVED FROM THE WATERS

Edinburgh, National Gallery of Scotland. Canvas, 200 × 339 cm.; about 1755–60.

Originally in the Palazzo Barbarigo at Venice, this picture was a pendant to Fontebasso's *Alexander and Diogenes*.

A figure of a halbardier has been cut from the right-hand side of the canvas and is now in the Tree Collection in London. There is an old copy of the Edinburgh picture in the Museum at Stuttgart.

Exhibited in London 1930.

73
APOLLO

London, Victoria and Albert Museum. Pen drawing with sepia washes, about 18 × 16 cm. 1757.

Many of the preparatory drawings for the frescoes in the Villa Valmarana are divided between the Victoria and Albert Museum and the Museo Civico in Trieste. This is a design for the group of *Apollo and Diana* in the Sala dell'Olimpo in the Foresteria.

74
DIANA

Stuttgart, Kupferstichkabinett. Pen drawing with sepia washes, 18 × 16 cm.; 1757.

A preliminary study for the same group as Plate 73.

Exhibited in Venice 1951.

75
SAINT THECLA DELIVERING THE CITY FROM THE PLAGUE

Este, Chiesa delle Grazie. Canvas, 675 × 390 cm.; 1759. Signed G. BATTA.TIEPOLO/F.

Generally considered to be one of Tiepolo's greatest masterpieces. On the 29th June, 1758, the City Council of Este decided to obtain the services of some excellent painter to paint an altarpiece representing St. Thecla as Protectress of Este. There is a letter of 1760 which records the placing of the picture on the High Altar on Christmas Eve, 1759. The altarpiece was engraved by Lorenzo Tiepolo. A modello is in the Metropolitan Museum, New York.

76
THE ANNUNCIATION

Paris, Private Collection. Pen drawing with sepia washes, 25 × 19.5 cm.; about 1760–70.

Almost Rembrandtesque in its chiaroscuro, this is one of Tiepolo's finest *Annunciations*.

Exhibited in Venice 1951.

77
THE TRIUMPH OF HERCULES

Verona, Palazzo Canossa. Fresco, 1761.

The Palazzo Canossa was built by the famous architect Michele Sanmicheli soon after 1527, and a new wing was built in 1760 for Carlo di Canossa, who also commissioned the fresco. The decoration of the great saloon is recorded in a poem of 1761 by Zaccaria Betti. From this poem we know that Tiepolo was assisted by the architect Pietro Visconti, and he also had the help of his son Domenico in painting the grisailles of the *Four Quarters of the Earth* and the five overdoors with allegories of the Virtues.

The ceiling fresco was badly damaged in 1945 at the time of the destruction of the Castelvecchio Bridge but the fragments have been replaced on the ceiling. The modello for this fresco was once in the Wertheim Collection in Berlin.

78
APOTHEOSIS OF THE PISANI FAMILY

Strà, Villa Pisani. Fresco, 23.50 × 13.50 m.; 1761–62.

The Villa Pisani was built about the middle of the eighteenth century by the Paduan architect Gerolamo Frigimelica. The decoration of the Grand Saloon was the last work executed by Tiepolo in Italy. On 10th May, 1760, he wrote from Venice to Count Algarotti saying that he was working on the modello for the Villa Pisani and that this work would keep him busy for three or four years. The modello he mentioned is now in the Museum at Angers. On 16th March, 1761, Tiepolo wrote again to Algarotti saying that he was painting in the Grand Saloon and on the 22nd December of the same year he was able to say that he was finishing many works including the Grand Saloon in the Villa Pisani. In the lower part of the fresco there are several amusing portraits of members of the Pisani family who have recently been identified.

79-90
FRESCOES IN THE THRONE ROOM OF THE ROYAL PALACE, MADRID

1762–64.

In December 1761, King Charles III of Spain commissioned Tiepolo to decorate the Royal Palace in Madrid, built by the Italian architect Giambattista Sacchetti. Tiepolo records the invitation in a letter of the 22nd December, 1761, which was written either to Algarotti or to Farsetti. On 30th January, 1762, the Duke of Montealegre, Spanish Ambassador in Venice, wrote that Tiepolo had promised to leave as soon as possible and on the 3rd April he recorded Tiepolo's departure. Tiepolo arrived in Madrid on 4th June, 1762, and set to work immediately. Before leaving Italy he had prepared a modello, which is certainly the large painting now in the National Gallery of Art at Washington.

On the ceiling of the throne room Tiepolo represented the *Apotheosis of Spain* (signed and dated 1764); on the ceiling of the Guard Room *Aeneas Conducted to the Temple of Venus* (1764–66), and on the ceiling of the Saleta the *Apotheosis of the Spanish Monarchy* (1764–66).

It used to be said that the *Aeneas* in the Guard Room (Fig. 58) was painted first, followed by the throne room and then by the Saleta (Fig. 59) but this must be wrong since the throne room is dated 1764 and we know that all the frescoes were finished at the end of 1766. On 16th January, 1767, after completing the fresco cycle Tiepolo agreed to remain in Spain.

The preparatory sketch for the *Apotheosis of Spain* is in Washington (Pls. 79, 81), and the two for the *Aeneas* are in Boston and Cambridge, Mass. (Figs. 57, 60). Two others for the *Apotheosis of the Spanish Monarchy* are in New York (one in the Metropolitan Museum and the other in the de Backer-Rothschild Collection).

91
S. FRANCIS

London, Count Seilern Collection. Canvas, 63 × 38 cm.; about 1767.

One of the modelletti for the seven altarpieces commissioned for the Church at Aranjuez. Four of these modelletti (S. Pascal, S. Francis, S. Charles and S. Joseph) are in the Seilern collection (Figs. 61–63), and another, for the *Immaculate Conception*, is in the collection of Lord Kinnaird in London. The sketch for *S. Peter of Alcantara* is lost and so is that for the *S. Anthony*, which seems once to have belonged to the painter Bayeu. Charles III commissioned the seven altarpieces in 1767 for the church at Aranjuez but they are now scattered over Europe and America. In a letter of 29th August, 1769, Tiepolo said that the canvases were completed; but in 1770, after Tiepolo's death, the altarpieces were removed and replaced by Neoclassical works by Mengs, Bayeu, and others. There is also a record of another picture painted for the dining-room of the Convent in Aranjuez representing the Blessed Andrès Ibernon but nothing further is known about it.

Exhibited in Venice 1951.

92
THE REST ON THE FLIGHT INTO EGYPT

Lisbon, Alice Ferreira Pinto-Basto Collection. Canvas, 55 × 41 cm.; about 1762–70.

In his last years Tiepolo painted a series of variations on the theme of the Flight into Egypt. We can see that this was a subject particularly dear to him from the many drawings which exist, as well as from the paintings which include one in Bellagio and one in a private collection in Berlin as well as these two in Lisbon, so different in composition and yet so close in their intimate feeling.

93
THE FLIGHT INTO EGYPT

Lisbon, Edoardo Ferreira Pinto-Basto Collection. Canvas, 57 × 43.5 cm.; about 1762–70.

The predominant element in this composition is the boat in the foreground, as those in many earlier drawings by Giambattista. Similar ideas were developed by Domenico Tiepolo in his 27 etchings published in 1753 under the title *Idee pittoresche sopra la Fuga in Egitto*.

NOTES ON THE COLOUR PLATES

I
TIEPOLO'S SELF-PORTRAIT WITH HIS SON DOMENICO

Würzburg, Residenz. Fresco, 1752–3.

At the left-hand side of the cornice surrounding the great fresco of *Olympus* over the staircase Tiepolo represented himself with his son Domenico and another painter, perhaps one of his assistants such as Urlaub or Roth (cf. Plate 68). This self-portrait in fresco is certainly the most vivid and intense that Tiepolo ever painted. Other self-portraits by him occur in the figure of the young Jacob in the scene of *Rachel hiding the idols* in the Archiepiscopal Palace of Udine; another, rather satirical, is in the Palazzo Clerici frescoes in Milan and yet another in the frescoes in Palazzo Labia in Venice. The artist in the *Apelles* (Colour Plate II) also has the features of Tiepolo. (See the note to Plates 54–68 for the whole cycle of the frescoes at Würzburg.)

II
ALEXANDER AND CAMPASPE IN THE STUDIO OF APELLES

Montreal, Museum of Fine Arts. Canvas, 54 × 74 cm.; about 1725.

The picture was formerly at Sigmaringen in Germany. Another version of the same subject, painted about ten years later, was recently acquired by the Louvre. On stylistic grounds this picture is certainly not later than 1725 and the self-portrait of Tiepolo as Apelles shows him still a young man.

Exhibited in Venice 1951.

IX. APOLLO PURSUING DAPHNE. Canvas, about 1755-60. Washington, National Gallery of Art (Samuel H. Kress Collection)

III

S. DOMINIC INSTITUTING THE ROSARY

Venice, Chiesa dei Gesuati. Fresco; 1737 to October, 1739.

The contract for the ceiling was drawn up in May, 1737 but there was a delay in the execution and the ceiling was not finished until October, 1739. Tiepolo's payment amounted to 12,400 Venetian lire. The frescoes on the ceiling are divided into three compartments, the one in the centre representing S. Dominic instituting the Rosary while the other two parts represent the Virgin hearing the prayers of the Saint and S. Dominic in Glory.
The modelletti for the *Institution of the Rosary* are in the Berlin Museum and the M. Crespi Collection in Milan, while the sketches for the smaller compartments are in the Johnson Collection, Philadelphia, and a private collection in America.

IV

DANAË

Stockholm, University Museum. Canvas, 41 × 53 cm.; just before 1736.

In 1736 the Count Tessin, the Swedish Minister in Venice, informed the Superintendent of the Royal Palace that he had bought some works by Tiepolo which arrived in Stockholm later. They included the *Decollation of St. John the Baptist* (Fig. 16) and the *Danaë*. This canvas was so popular in Sweden that at least four copies of it have been discovered there since the end of the 19th century, while other contemporary copies are in Italy.

Exhibited in Venice, 1951.

V

S. AGATHA

Berlin, Kaiser Friedrich Museum. See the note to Plate 51.

VI

'AMERICA'

Würzburg, Residenz. Fresco, 1752–3.

This is part of the group symbolizing America which is frescoed on the ceiling of the staircase.

America is personified by a splendid and opulent woman with a multi-coloured feathered head-dress carrying a bow on her shoulders and wearing large golden medals. She is seated on the back of a huge alligator and surrounded by a crowd of fantastic figures symbolizing the people of the whole continent.

For the fresco cycle in Würzburg see the note to Plates 53–68.

VII

THE MARRIAGE OF BARBAROSSA

Würzburg, Residenz. Fresco, 1752.

This scene frescoed on the wall of the Kaisersaal has been conceived as a sort of stage performance. In the old cathedral of Würzburg to which Tiepolo gave the architectural features of Palladio's style (the figures wear the costumes painted by Veronese), the Bishop Gebhard, Count of Hennerberg, blesses the marriage between the Emperor and Beatrice of Burgundy in the presence of a large crowd.

For the fresco cycle in Würzburg see the note to Plates 54–68.

VIII

SAINT THECLA DELIVERING THE CITY OF ESTE FROM THE PLAGUE

New York, Metropolitan Museum of Art. Canvas, 80 × 45 cm.; 1758.

This is the sketch for the altarpiece in the Chiesa delle Grazie in Este (Plate 75). By comparison with the finished altarpiece the modello shows a number of variations: in the background the view of Este has been almost entirely changed and the sketch does not have the dramatic incident of the carrying away of the corpse of a plague victim. Another sketch, by an imitator, is in a private collection in Paris and a drawing for the group of God the Father with the Angels was also formerly in the Orloff Collection, Paris.

Exhibited in New York 1938, and Venice 1951.

IX

APOLLO PURSUING DAPHNE

Washington, National Gallery of Art (Samuel H. Kress Collection). Canvas, 69.3 × 87.5 cm.; about 1755–60.

Signed at the lower left corner: G. B. Tiepolo. The picture dates from the same period as the frescoes in the Villa Valmarana at Vicenza (1757), for it recalls the style of that cycle (Figs. 47–50) and in particular the group of Apollo and Luna in the Foresteria, for which Tiepolo used the same models. The colours are fresh and light. The traditional iconography of the Metamorphosis is here treated in quite a new composition.

LIST OF TEXT ILLUSTRATIONS

37. *Rinaldo in the Garden of Armida.* Canvas, 39 × 62 cm. About 1755–60. Berlin, Gallery

38. *Rinaldo abandons Armida.* Canvas, 39 × 61 cm. About 1755–60. Paris, Cailleux Collection

39. *Armida crowning the sleeping Rinaldo with flowers; Armida and Rinaldo with a mirror.* Two canvases, each 134 × 72.5 cm. About 1750–55. New York, Private Collection

40. *The Adoration of the Magi.* Canvas, 60.4 × 47.6 cm. About 1753. New York, Metropolitan Museum

41. *The death of Hyacinth.* Canvas, 287 × 235 cm. About 1752–53. Lugano, Thyssen Collection

42. *Reception of the Emperor Henry III at the Villa Contarini.* Fresco, 4.02 × 7.29 m. 1755–56. Paris, Musée Jacquemart-André

43. *The Triumph of Faith.* Ceiling fresco, 1754–55. Venice, Chiesa della Pietà

44. *Apotheosis of the Soderini Family.* Ceiling fresco, about 1754. Destroyed in 1917, formerly in the Villa Soderini-Berti at Nervesa

45. Giandomenico Tiepolo: *The Charlatan.* Fresco, 1757. Vicenza, Villa Valmarana

46. Giandomenico Tiepolo: *The Diorama.* Fresco, 1757. Vicenza, Villa Valmarana

47. *Mars and Venus.* Fresco, 1757. Vicenza, Villa Valmarana

48. *Venus abandons Aeneas.* Fresco, 1757, Vicenza, Villa Valmarana

49. *The Sacrifice of Iphigenia.* Fresco, 1757. Vicenza, Villa Valmarana

50. *Apollo and Diana.* Fresco, 1757. Vicenza, Villa Valmarana

51. *The Triumph of Truth.* Fresco, about 1757. Destroyed in 1945, formerly, Vicenza, Palazzo Trento-Valmarana

52. *Merit between Nobility and Virtue.* Ceiling fresco, about 1758. Venice, Palazzo Rezzonico

53. *The Assumption of the Virgin.* Ceiling fresco, 1759. Udine, Chiesa della Purità

54. *Marriage Allegory.* Ceiling fresco, about 1758. Venice, Palazzo Rezzonico

55. *Allegorical figure.* Grisaille on canvas, 82 × 65 cm. About 1750–60. Zurich, Private Collection

56. *The Entombment.* Canvas, 57 × 43 cm. About 1762–70. Lisbon, Pinto Basto Collection

57. *Apotheosis of Aeneas.* Canvas, 66 × 50 cm. Sketch, about 1764–66. Boston, Museum of Fine Arts

58. *Apotheosis of Aeneas.* Fresco, 1764–66. Madrid, Royal Palace, Guard Room

59. *Apotheosis of the Spanish Monarchy.* Fresco, 1764–66. Madrid, Royal Palace, Saleta

60. *Apotheosis of Aeneas.* Canvas, 71 × 51 cm. Sketch, about 1764–66. Cambridge, Mass., Fogg Art Museum

61. *Saint Charles Borromeo.* Canvas, 63 × 38 cm. Sketch, between 1767 and 1769. London, Count Seilern Collection

62. *Saint Joseph.* Canvas, 63 × 38 cm. Sketch, between 1767 and 1769. London, Count Seilern Collection

63. *Saint Pascal Baylon.* Canvas, 63 × 38 cm. Sketch, between 1767 and 1769. London, Count Seilern Collection

64. *Saint James of Compostela.* Canvas, 317 × 162 cm. Altarpiece, about 1767–70. Budapest, Museum of Fine Arts